SUCCESS PRINCIPLES
FROM THE LIPS OF JESUS

Success Principles From the Lips of Jesus

by Dave Williams

"Give your servant success today. . . ." (Nehemiah 1:11b NIV)

GOOD GROUND BOOKS
P.O. Box 17115
Lansing, Michigan 48901

"And other fell on Good Ground . . . and bare fruit an hundredfold . . ." — Luke 8:8

First Printing 1980

ISBN: 0-938020-00-5

Printed in the United States of America

GOOD GROUND BOOKS

Dedicated To

My precious wife, Mary Jo, whose love and dedication has doubled my usefulness in the ministry.

Gary Uptigrove and Beverly Hopp for excellence in manuscript review.

Pastor E. Glenn Snook who has helped and encouraged me more than he realizes.

My faithful staff and partners who have stood by me in the good times and the rough.

Grateful Acknowledgements

Phillips, 1958, 1959, 1960, 1972. Published by
Macmillan Publishing Company, New York, N.Y.
Used by permission.

Special thanks to Bible Voice Incorporated,
Van Nuys, California, for their authorization to
use quotes from the book *Terror at Tenerife,*
copyright 1977. This is the inside story of history's
worst airline disaster as told to George Otis by Norman Williams.

All other Scripture quotations used in this book
are taken from the King James Version.

Psalm 68:11

"THE LORD GAVE THE WORD: GREAT WAS THE COMPANY OF THOSE THAT PUBLISHED IT." The following is a list of our "associate publishers" to whom we are deeply grateful.

(* indicates a memorial gift)

M. Liz Wilson
Joseph J. Tomanica*
Lester (Bud) Williams*
Trina Lee Williams
Chuck Tomanica
Mr. & Mrs. Ken Holmberg
Mr. & Mrs. John Hall
Debbie Wilson
Bob Wilson, Jr.
Connie Denslow
Sheila Wilson
Joseph V. Covello
Mary Julia Sipka*
John Paul Sipka*
Harold L. Lemon
Leona B. Lemon*
William E. Lemon*
Harvey Sheets
Sheila Cole
Michael Tomanica

Gary & Patti Uptigrove
Larry Tomanica
Iva Troyer
Rocky & Tony Troyer
Rocky Barra
Tom Basham
Don & Mary Mooney
Tim & Char Tomanica
Kathy Clark
Jon & Pat Eyer
Lou & Lil Sipka
Susan Kay Sipka
Doug & Debbie Williams
Craig Cole
Dave & Laura Andrew
Beverly Hopp
Ann Hicks
Sue Hoisington
Mary Sipka
Frank & Jeri Thomas

HOW THIS BOOK WILL HELP YOU

This book will help you to learn some of the basic principles for successful living. As you read these pages, you will find that the principles taught herein will apply to every situation in life, regardless of what it may be:

. . . a more harmonious marriage.
. . . a more effective soul-winning program.
. . . an improved business.
. . . finding the job you really want.
. . . experiencing greater success in the ministry.
. . . getting along better with other people.
. . . receiving God's direction for your life.
. . . bringing glory to your Heavenly Father.

Applying these simple teachings of Jesus, you will be able to step up from the pits of defeat, and into the arena of victory living.

— D.W.

Table of Contents

Introduction

SUCCESS! For years I tried to establish success in my own life. But it seemed as though everything I set my hand to failed. Oh, I never had any trouble finding employment, but whenever I tried my "luck" at going into business for myself, I flopped. I was beginning to wonder if my middle name was spelled F-A-I-L-U-R-E.

My record company went "down the tube." My security form agency never got off the ground and my mail order jewelry enterprise was a fiasco! What was I doing wrong?

In spite of my long string of defeats, I just couldn't bring myself to believe that failure was an accident. Nor could I accept the so-called fact that success was only for the "lucky ones" whose numbers happened to come up on the great roulette wheel in the sky. There had to be a way, I thought, to succeed in a world of plenty. Others

1

were doing it, why couldn't I?

Then it happened! One morning I met a Man who changed my life. His name: Jesus Christ. He's the greatest example of success that ever lived. Reading and studying His Word transformed my thinking from poverty to prosperity; from sickness to health; from darkness to light; from the temporal to the eternal. I discovered that Jesus Christ came to give me an abundant life, not a life of defeat and poverty. I began to realize that "luck" had nothing to do with a person's success. The Lord revealed to me from His Word that sin, sickness, and poverty were under the curse of the Law, and JESUS CHRIST HAD REDEEMED ME FROM THE CURSE OF THE LAW (Galatians 3:13).

When I learned that Jesus was willing to give me the power to fulfill God's command to "be fruitful," my whole life drastically changed. Instead of failing, I began to succeed. Instead of experiencing poverty, I began to prosper. Instead of suffering continual sickness, I stepped up to divine health.

Your life will change too! You will begin to succeed where you've failed before as you put into practice the principles of success taught in the Bible. So prepare to taste a new dimension of living you never dreamed possible.

Join me now as we travel through the pages of God's Word, discovering SUCCESS PRINCIPLES FROM THE LIPS OF JESUS.

— D.W.

CHAPTER ONE

YOUR SUCCESS PRINCIPLE
FOR TODAY:

Be Guided By God!

TEXT: *Whoever follows Me will never walk in darkness, but will have the Light of Life* (John 8:12 NIV).

Have you ever been faced with making a challenging decision? Have you ever been confronted with two choices and not known which to pick? Have you wanted to walk in God's plan for your life, but somehow staggered in the dark, not knowing which path to take? Well, there is good news for you!

The good news is this: Whoever follows Jesus will never walk in darkness. Many people fail to claim that promise for their lives. Consequently, they still bear the darkness of confusion, indecision, anxiety, and frustration.

You and I *can* be successful. But we can't do it apart from the guidance of God. Without God's direction in our lives, we can't even hope to be suc-

4

cessful.

The VICTORY PERSON has learned that God *wants* to guide his footsteps (Psalm 32:8). He understands that the Lord is delighted to direct the affairs of his life and crown his efforts with success (Proverbs 3:6 TLB).

Jesus said, "My sheep listen to my voice; I know them and THEY FOLLOW ME" (John 10:27 NIV). Following Jesus is a key to living the victorious life.

In order to experience the success God has for us, we must learn a few things about God's guidance.

1. We must learn to recognize the voice of Jesus.
2. We must listen to the voice of Jesus.
3. We must follow His instructions.

Jesus never tells us to do something just because He delights in bossing us around. No, no, no! Everything Jesus tells us is always for our own benefit and invariably points us in the direction of victory.

OBEYING THE WORDS OF JESUS

One day while teaching in the synagogue, Jesus noticed a man that had a withered hand. He spoke to the man, "Stretch forth thine hand!" The man followed Jesus' command and immediately was healed. You see, it was to the man's own profit to comply with Jesus' instructions. His obedience was exercised to his own advantage. (See Mark 3:1-5.)

Following the instructions of Jesus paid off on another occasion. Jesus told some fishermen to launch out into the deep waters and let down their nets if they wanted to catch a lot of fish. Someone spoke up and informed Jesus that they had been fishing all night and hadn't caught a single fish. At first, it looked as though they weren't going to listen to His command, but finally one of them spoke up and said, "Because You say so, we'll try again."

They did try again. They acted on Jesus' words and let down their nets in the deep waters. This time the nets were so full of fish they began to tear at the seams! The men even had to call another boat for help. They followed the guidance of Jesus and prospered because of it. (Read Luke 5:1-7.)

God wants to fill our "nets" to overflowing. But we must accept and act upon His direction in our lives. We don't need to stumble in the dark when we have the Light of Life guiding our footsteps to successful living!

HOW DO WE RECEIVE THIS GUIDANCE FROM GOD TODAY?

In order to accurately learn the voice of Jesus, we must first learn what the Bible says. We all must learn God's character, God's purposes, s principles, and God's general will for our lives. We learn these things from the Word of God. It must be understood that the Lord will never violate nor contradict His Written Word. That's why it's vitally important to learn God's voice there first.

> "For ever O Lord, thy word is settled in heaven" (Psalm 119:89).

> "Heaven and earth will pass away: but MY WORDS shall not pass away" — Jesus (Mark 13:31).

God will never contradict His Written Word. It is forever settled. It can't be changed or altered. We must not add to It or take away from It lest we fall under a solemn judgement (Revelation 22:18, 19).

A LADY WHO FELT CALLED TO THE MISSION FIELD

I talked with a lady a few years ago who failed to discern God's voice because of her lack of Bible knowledge. Sadly enough, I was unable to help her. Having her mind made up, she was determined to travel to a distant land to work as a missionary. She claimed that God had called her to do this even if it meant divorcing her husband and making the journey with only her three-year-old son.

Thinking God had spoken to her, she persisted in her delusion. She said she would get to that country no matter who she had to step on or step over to get there. Had she taken the time to learn God's character, perhaps this tragic event could have been avoided. But she didn't. Separating from her husband, she left for another country to do "God's work."

What was the result? First, a ruined marriage. Her obligation to her husband was of a higher priority in God's eyes than going to the mission field. Next, three damaged human lives. A man's wife gets a notion and leaves! What's the husband to do now? Then, the child — what about him? How do you tell a three-year-old that "God" wanted Mommy to get rid of Daddy so she could be a missionary? All this destruction because one person with an unteachable spirit, persisted in following a demon-inspired idea.

This sort of thing happens quite often to those individuals who operate their lives by "feelings" and "impressions" alone, apart from the Written Word of God. The Bible is more sure than any prophecy, voice, dream, feeling, or impression that may emerge upon us. We are always safe when acting according to God's Written Word.

ANOTHER LADY WHO FELT "CALLED" TO LEAVE HER HUSBAND

About a year ago, a Christian lady with whom I am personally acquainted, nearly made a tragic mistake by trusting her "impressions" instead of God's Word. She believed that God had spoken to her and told her that she was to leave her husband, divorce him, and marry a certain younger fellow. Interestingly enough, "the Lord had spoken" also to the young man and "told" him the same thing . . . so he said.

When friends learned about this unfortunate situation, they immediately began to pray. Thank God, He intervened and brought these misguided individuals to their spiritual senses before it was too late.

We would save ourselves a great deal of time and trouble if we would only give heed to the Written Word of God, the Bible.

GUIDANCE IN THE MIDST OF TRAGEDY

Norman Williams knows the guidance of God. He knows what it means to follow the Light of Life — Jesus. He was aboard one of the two 747 airliners that crashed on the Canary Islands in 1977. Five hundred and eighty-one people perished in that holocaust, but Brother Williams was miraculously guided from the burning aircraft.

"Blood-curdling screams of people being burned alive were mixed with the cries of people calling for their loved ones, moans, curses, and other indescribable sounds of human agony and rage."*

Norman was brought up to know the Word of God. As people were dying all around him, he envisioned himself back at home holding the Bible with his mother. He knew the Written Word of God and received guidance from It during this dreadful time of terror.

". . . When thou walkest through the fire, thou shalt not be burned; neither shall the flame kindle upon thee" (Isaiah 43:2).

Claiming the Promise of God, Brother Williams screamed out, "IN THE NAME OF JESUS, THROUGH YOUR SHED BLOOD, I STAND ON YOUR WORD!"*

Instantly, as he claimed the Promise from the Written Word of God, he began to move through the heaving, exploding havoc. Jesus Christ guided him safely out and away from the dying aircraft.

Today, Norman Williams is traveling across the country, sharing the Good News of Jesus Christ and telling people everywhere, "GOD'S WORD WORKS!"

Get to know God in His Word. That's where

---

*Taken from the book *Terror at Tenerife* by Norman Williams as told to George Otis. Published 1977 by Bible Voice, Inc., Van Nuys, California 91409. Used by permission of the publisher.

you will genuinely grow to know God better and learn His voice. Then you will be able to discern that which is from God, and that which is not. Only you can make the decision to allow your life to be guided by God's Word. You don't have to walk in darkness, if you will follow the Light of Life — Jesus Christ — through His Word.

WHAT ABOUT SPECIFIC SITUATIONS?

What about more specific situations? It's one thing to learn God's general guidance from His Word, but quite another to receive distinct, concrete, detailed direction for special circumstances. Let's take a look at some of the more specific areas of our lives the Lord wants to guide.

BUSINESS REALM

Jesus wants to guide our lives in every area. This includes our job, our business, our ministry, our finances — EVERYTHING! And, of course, having made Jesus Christ the Lord of our lives, we *want* Him to guide every area of our lives.

I know of a particular businessman who had very little formal education. He did, however, have the schooling of the Holy Spirit and applied himself to learning the principles of God's guidance. No deals would be negotiated and no contracts would be signed by this Christian businessman without FIRST learning the mind of the Lord on the matter. He refused to make any major decision without FIRST receiving guidance from God. He would pray and wait. If no answer came immediately, he'd hold off on all pending transactions until the answer came and was confirmed. This is the way he operated the business. Jesus was in control. Today, this man is a multimillionaire, and is being used of God in helping to financially support various aspects of God's work in the world.

> ". . . Let the Lord be magnified, which hath pleasure in the prosperity of his servant" (Psalm 35:27).

> ". . . No good thing will he withhold from them that walk uprightly" (Psalm 84:11).

IN PREACHING AND TEACHING

Something we preachers and teachers need to burn into our thinking is this:

WE WOULD MINISTER TO PEOPLE MUCH MORE EFFECTIVELY AND FRUITFULLY IF WE'D ALLOW EACH OF OUR MESSAGES TO BE GUIDED BY GOD.

No, I don't mean to say that we shouldn't prepare and use notes — that's part of our armor, "the *preparation* of the gospel of peace," — but I *do* mean to say that as we prepare, we should remain sensitive to the Lord's leading. (This goes for Sunday School teachers too!)

Some time ago, I received an invitation to speak at an out-of-town gathering. After praying about it and seeking the Lord's counsel, I was certain that God wanted me to accept this engagement, so I did.

"What do you want me to teach about, Lord?" I asked. "Please reveal to me what the people's needs are so that I can minister to them more profitably."

There was absolutely no immediate, specific guidance from the Lord. So I waited. Admittedly, I became a bit anxious and started poring over some of the messages I had given at other speaking engagements, but the Holy Spirit didn't give His witness in my heart about any of them. So I waited some more.

A minister usually likes to spend six to eight hours preparing for a sermon or a teaching lesson, but in this case it was different. Only a few hours before I was to address that congregation, the Lord moved upon my heart to examine the subject of "Developing the Mind and Attitude of Christ." No matter what else I would try to think about, my mind kept returning to "Developing the Mind and Attitude of Christ," so I sat down at my desk and began to meditate on the subject. As I did, the Lord began to reveal to me from His Word how we can develop in our lives the same mind and attitude that Christ had. I began to write things as they came to my mind. In an hour, perhaps a little less, God had given to me from His Word the message I was to share that evening.

Five minutes before the service was to begin, I walked into the building where I was scheduled to speak. As I stepped into the hall, a young man asked me the question, "Are you Mr. Williams?"

"Yes," I answered.

He then proceeded to share something with me. In the process he said, "I sure hope you will be able to help me. You see, I've been having a real struggle with my attitude. I have a bad attitude and need to learn how to develop a good one."

At that point I began to rejoice in my spirit because I knew that this man would be helped and encouraged that night as I shared the Word of God on "How to Develop the Mind and Attitude of Christ." There was no question that God had given me that message. He confirmed it in the hearts and lives of the people in that congregation that night.

We preachers and teachers need not grope in the dark for effective messages if we are following the Light of Life — Jesus.

Of course, some ministers and Sunday School teachers are "too busy" to pray and seek God's counsel and guidance about the lessons. That's why they remain unsuccessful. That's the reason they "win a few — lose a few," and KEEP ONLY A *VERY FEW!*

GUIDANCE IN SELECTING STAFF MEMBERS

If we are to be successful in our call in life, we must follow Jesus. Following His example goes right along with following Him. We should study the Life of our Lord, consider the way He did things, and do them that way ourselves.

For example, before Jesus asked anyone to be a part of His apostolic team, He spent the entire night in prayer. Undoubtedly He was receiving direction from His Father in Heaven (Luke 6:12). Until the Father revealed to Him who the right person was for the right job, Jesus asked no one to assume any staff responsibilities.

Jesus was guided by the Holy Spirit at all times. He never functioned independently of the Father's guidance. Neither should we, lest we be guilty of the sin of presumption.

> "Keep back thy servant also from presumptuous sins . . ." (Psalm 19:13).

PROTECTION

God is speaking. Jesus Christ is trying to guide our lives by the Holy Spirit. As His children, we can develop our "inner man" to the place where we can recognize God's voice. We can progress in our spiritual lives to the place where we become more and more in tune with God's Spirit. But it won't happen by filling our lives with unprofitable television programs and other time-wasting activities. It will happen by giving diligence in applying our hearts to God's Word. This is where we first learn to recognize the direction of God in our lives.

Ray Trask, an Assembly of God missionary in Indonesia, shared an interesting account with us which I'd like to share with you.

In Indonesia, being sensitive to God's voice is sometimes a matter of life and death. One day Ray flew to a particular island to visit with a native pastor whom some of the non-Christian island dwellers were constantly trying to murder. As Ray and the native pastor sat in a restaurant, the Lord spoke to the pastor and said, "THERE IS POISON IN YOUR TEA. DON'T DRINK IT!" So he obeyed the Lord. Later it was discovered that indeed there was poison in the tea and had he drunk it, death may have resulted. Acting upon the direction of God, his life was spared.

SOME METHODS OF GOD'S GUIDANCE

You may be asking the question, "But, what are some of the methods that God uses to guide His people?" We will take a brief look at some of the methods of God's guidance.

1. *The Written Word of God.* The Bible is always the first and foremost place to go for direction from God. All other forms of guidance are subject to this (Psalm 119:105; John 8:31, 32; Luke 6:47, 48; Mark 12:24).

2. *Counselors.* Spiritually mature counselors will be able to help you to some degree. But don't ask the advice or opinions of people you know to be generally negative and unspiritual. Make certain your counselors are people who are close to Jesus (Proverbs 15:22).

3. *Inner Guidance of the Holy Spirit.* This is where God works "in you" to do His will. He gives you the right desires as you are seeking Him first (Philippians 2:13; Hebrews 13:20, 21; Acts 11:12).

4. *Mouth of Two or Three Witnesses.* When you think God is moving you in a certain direction, ask Him to confirm it by two or three reasonable, reliable, sensible individuals (Deuteronomy 17:6; Matthew 18:16; 2 Corinthians 13:1).

5. *Dreams or Visions.* Be cautious here. If a dream or a vision is from God, the meaning will be crystal clear. There will be no strange, mystical, hidden meaning (Matthew 1:20, 2:12; Acts 9:10, 16:9, 18:9).

6. *Prophecy or Word of Knowledge.* Never accept an oral utterance exclusively for direction; only confirmation. In other words, an oral gift of the Spirit should never be accepted as your only source of direction. They may, however, confirm something that the Lord has already been dealing with you about (Acts 13:1-3).

7. *The Peace of God.* God's peace will always rule in your heart when you are moving in His will. There will never be an uncertain agitation or unrest in your spirit when you are being directed by God. He will give you His peace, thus assuring you that you are making the right move (Philippians 4:7-9).

8. *Sanctified Common Sense.* God never asks you to do foolish things that serve no purpose. Beware of individuals who are always doing some unintelligent, preposterous thing and blaming it on the Lord (Proverbs 3:21).

SOME IMPORTANT FACTS ABOUT FOLLOWING GOD:

1. *God Usually Does Not Reveal to Us Every Step From Beginning to End.* He will guide us one step at a time. As we are obedient to follow step number one, He will, at the right time, guide us to step number two, step number three, and so forth.

"The steps of a good man are ordered by the Lord: and he delighteth in his way" (Psalm 37:23).

2. *We Must Be Close To God to Receive His Clear Guidance.* Our ministry produces a radio program which is transmitted from a station in St. Johns, Michigan. When you are in that city, the program is received clearly, however, the farther away you drive, the fuzzier the reception becomes. Go farther yet and the broadcast fades out, then back in, then back out again. Soon the signal is so distorted that you're not even sure if you're on the right channel or not.

That's what happens to us the farther away from God we get. The signals start becoming fuzzy and distorted. Other voices begin to bleed in. Soon, we're not sure if we are hearing from God, the devil, or our own imaginations.

When this happens, and confusion begins to set in, that's the time to cancel the dinner engagements, postpone the business meeting, and get alone with God for a time of prayer and meditation. Draw near to God through His Word, prayer, and faith. Then make the decision to STAY close to the Lord. That's the real key — staying close to God. Make walking with God a way of life.

"Come near to God and He will come near to you" (James 4:8 NIV).

"But if we walk in the light, as he is in the light, we have fellowship one with another . . ." (I John 1:7).

3. *We Must Continue in God's Word.* The Bible is the Christian's Supreme Court to which there is no appeal. All forms of guidance are subject to God's Written Word. There are no exceptions.

". . . If ye continue in my word, then are ye my disciples indeed; And ye shall know the truth, and the truth shall make you free" (John 8:31, 32).

A person can expect God to lead and guide his life if he will but stay faithful to the task of following Jesus through His Word.

If we desire to be successful, we must allow ourselves to be directed by the Light of Life — JESUS CHRIST. It is through Him that the darkness is expelled and we begin to walk in the Light.

IN QUICK REVIEW:

1. To be successful, we must: (a) learn to recognize the voice of Jesus (b) listen to the voice of Jesus (c) follow Jesus.

2. In order to accurately learn the voice of Jesus, we must be willing to learn the Bible.

3. Methods of guidance: (a) Bible (b) Counselors (c) Inner guidance (d) two or three witnesses (e) dreams or visions (f) gifts of Spirit (g) peace of God (h) sanctified common sense.

4. Facts about following God: (a) take one step at a time (b) stay close to God (c) continue in His Word.

YOUR SUCCESS PRINCIPLE FOR TODAY: FOLLOW JESUS — BE GUIDED BY GOD.

CHAPTER TWO

YOUR SUCCESS PRINCIPLE
FOR TODAY:

Quit Procrastinating!

TEXT: *"As long as it is day, we must do the work of Him Who sent Me. Night is coming, when no one can work"* (John 9:4 NIV).

"Tomorrow, I'm going to make things right."

"Next week, I'm going to look for a job."

"Someday, I'm going to be a soulwinner!"

"When I have more time, I'll come to your church."

"I'll get organized next week."

"I'll accept Jesus Christ someday, but not right now. The conditions aren't right."

"One of these days, I'll get this house cleaned up."

We have all heard, and perhaps even made, statements such as these at one time or another in our lives, but few people realize the grave consequences of putting things off. Every time a person delays a decision or action that could be executed immediately, he is sowing the seeds of a dreadfully destructive habit called . . . PROCRASTINA- TION!

Procrastination is the developed habit of put- ting things off until a more "convenient" time or season. This is what Felix did after St. Paul had ex- plained to him about righteousness, self-control, and the coming judgement.

". . . When I have a convenient season, I will call for thee" — Felix (Acts 24:25).

There is no record of Felix ever finding his more "convenient season."

Jesus indicated that there is coming a time when it will be too late to do the tasks assigned to us. We must "work while it is day," for "night is coming" and all work will come to an end.

NOW FAITH IS . . .

"Now faith is . . ." (Hebrews 11:1). Faith is *now*. We cannot hope to have great faith for proj- ects and plans in the future if we fail to exercise our faith *now*. Faith is not something to practice "someday." Faith is not something to begin "tomorrow." Faith is always *NOW!*

With faith, we can make proper decisions and take essential actions immediately when necessary.

We don't have to continually put things off until a "more convenient season."

Faith is like muscle. When fed properly (Romans 10:17) and given the necessary exercise (James 2:17, 26), it will grow. If it's not fed properly and exercised adequately, it will diminish.

The spiritual law of use/atrophy is at work. If we use what we have, more will be added. However, if we fail to use what has been given, even what we have will be lost.

> ". . . With the measure you use, it will be measured to you — and even more; whoever does not have, even what he has will be taken from him" (Mark 4:24-25 NIV).

Procrastination is an enemy of faith. Many people have allowed this habit to develop in their lives. Instead of putting action to their faith, they hesitate at making decisions, and put off setting up plans. They delay; they hang back; they hold off; they stall; and, as a result, their lives seem to go around in circles. Facing the same trials and problems month after month, year after year, they never learn how to effectively combat and gain victory over them. The pages of our history books are filled with records of how entire battles were lost, all because somebody dragged their feet in making a decision and taking action.

Procrastination is a hindrance to success. It's a standard enemy that each of us must master if we are to experience genuine victory.

A CASE OF PROCRASTINATION

Some time ago, I *felt* as though I had done wrong to a certain minister friend of mine. He hadn't called me in a long while, and I hadn't seen him in several weeks, so I *assumed* he was perturbed with me. I didn't know why but the devil was slick in manufacturing quite a number of reasons. Instead of calling the man right away, I allowed these various negative thoughts to eat away at my mind. It began to affect my teaching, writing, and thinking in general. Every time I would try to study or do some spiritual work, the feeling would grip me that I had caused this minister considerable distress.

"Should I call him?"

"Should I wait for him to call me?"

"What should I do?"

This persisted for several weeks. It was tormenting me! I was torn between two or three possible modes of action and couldn't decide which to take.

Finally, I said to myself, "This is ridiculous! I'll just call the guy and get it over with. If he's upset with me about something, I'll make it right with him. If not, I'll no longer be bothered by these apprehensive thoughts."

I dialed his number. In a few moments he and I were on the phone together, sharing how much we appreciated each other's ministry. He wasn't sore at me in the least. In fact, he apologized for not calling me.

In just one minute of time, my mind was cleared, the anxiety was lifted, and a relationship was restored. Because of the sin of procrastination, I had wasted all those weeks worrying about something that wasn't true. I had allowed my mind to become infected with uneasiness and needless concern, simply because I failed to make the decision to call this person; I kept putting it off.

LEADERSHIP

One of the chief qualities of a good leader is decisiveness. Notice the outstanding characteristics of leaders in the Bible. Among these attributes is the quality of being able to conquer the sin of procrastination and to arrive at decisions promptly.

When Absolom plotted to overthrow his father's kingdom, messengers brought the facts concerning this conspiracy to David. Immediately, David made a decision to take action. He didn't dilly-dally around and entertain thoughts of fear and worry! HE ACTED PROMPTLY UPON THE FACTS! (2 Samuel 15:13, 14)

The person who cannot overcome the success-destroying practice of procrastination will most likely never be an outstanding leader. This one habit has kept thousands of otherwise qualified individuals from holding leadership positions.

On the other hand, the person who learns to make prompt, accurate decisions will begin to see "mountains" moving aside to make room for him. He knows where he's going and he moves ahead uncompromisingly.

DOUBLE-MINDEDNESS

All through life there are decisions we will be required to make. The double-minded man loses all the way around because he makes no firm decisions, and making *no decision* is actually making *a submission* . . . to failure! The Bible clearly states:

> "For let not that man think that he shall receive any thing of the Lord. A double minded man is unstable in all his ways" (James 1:7-8).

To illustrate the destructive effect of being double-minded, I will share this story with you:

> During the Civil War, a young soldier couldn't make up his mind which side to be on. In his double-mindedness, he "decided" to be friends with both sides by wearing a Confederate jacket and Yankee trousers. But Yankee soldiers shot him in the chest and Confederate soldiers shot him in the legs!

Double mindedness and indecision will almost always guarantee failure.

Years ago, I sat in a state of confusion in my living room, not knowing which way to turn. I knew that God had His hand upon my life and I had a tremendous desire to serve Him in a fuller capacity, but just didn't know where to begin. I sat there on the floor in a frustrated state of mind. I had tried serving the Lord in various ways, but everything spelled F-A-I-L-U-R-E!

I picked up my Bible. Reading it, I came to James 1:5-8 — "If any of you lack wisdom . . ." (Well, that certainly described me; I lacked wisdom!) ". . . Let him ask of God, that giveth to all men liberally, and upbraideth not, and it shall be given him." At this point I got excited. I grabbed the Living Bible and read it there also. Here's what it said:

> "If you want to know what God wants you to do, ask Him, and He will gladly tell you, for He is always ready to give a bountiful supply of wisdom to all who ask Him; He will not resent it. But when you ask Him, be sure that you really expect Him to tell you, for a doubtful mind will be as unsettled as a wave of the sea that is driven and tossed by the wind; And every decision you then make will be uncertain, as you first turn this way, and then that. If you don't ask with faith, don't expect the Lord to give you any solid answer" (James 1:5-8 TLB).

This was precisely what I needed! I wanted to know what God wanted me to do and this was the way to find out. So I prayed, "Father, in Jesus'

Name, I ask you to let me know what you want me
to do. What is my calling in life, Lord? Thank you
for answering. Amen.''

Then I remained very quiet for a few moments.
Words from the Bible gently began to rise up in my
spirit. It was from Jeremiah: ''I have called you to
speak My Word and to speak it faithfully'' (Jeremiah 23:28). I then spoke those words with my
mouth, ''I have called you to speak My Word and
to speak it faithfully.'' I repeated it again; this time
with so much enthusiasm and excitement I could
hardly contain myself! I was so happy, and *now* I
never doubt what God has called me to do.

''Call unto me, and I will answer thee . . .''
(Jeremiah 33:3).

Later I discovered that many people in the Bible
asked God specific questions and received specific
answers. (See Judges 20:18-29; I Samuel 10:20-22;
II Samuel 2:1, 5:19, 23; I Chronicles 14:10, 13-16;
II Corinthians 12:8-9.)

We all face seemingly complex situations from
time to time. Common sense is good in decision
making, but oftentimes not good enough. We need
SUPERNATURAL WISDOM from Someone
Who sees the whole scope of things; beginning and
ending. This Person, Jesus Christ, will give wisdom
GENEROUSLY to all who will ask for it in faith.

WHY DO WE PUT OFF MAKING DECISIONS AND TAKING ACTIONS?

1. *Fear.* We are afraid we might make the wrong move. We fail to trust our actions into the hands of a Loving Heavenly Father.

2. *Feelings.* Let's face it. Some days we just plain don't feel like making decisions or taking actions. Some days we don't feel like working, or like moving ahead toward our goals. We sometimes don't feel like apologizing to somebody we have wronged.

    Well, the VICTORY PERSON has learned to operate his life NOT merely by what his feelings tell him, but more importantly, by what the Bible tells him. He does what's right whether he feels like it or not.

3. *Not Knowing How to Break the Habit of Procrastination.* Do you want to break the habit of putting things off? Let's take a look at how to do it.

    First of all, if you want to gain mastery over this victory impairing habit, you must start by making the change immediately! That means RIGHT NOW! If you say, "Maybe I'll quit procrastinating tomorrow," you are a double-minded person and will most likely never experience real success in your life. The change has to begin now.

For example, if you are overweight and have been putting off changing your eating habits, then you must decide RIGHT NOW — THIS VERY MOMENT — that you are going to make the change. Not tomorrow; *NOW!* Or perhaps you are one who always postpones the unpleasant tasks until the end of the day. Then they pile up and put you under a tremendous strain when you finally force yourself to do them. Well, this is your day to change.

Secondly, don't try to do everything at once. Perhaps there are many decisions you have failed to make and several actions you have been neglecting. Try compelling yourself RIGHT NOW to make one decision or take one action you've been putting off. Then, starting the first thing tomorrow, begin to make a plan for doing all the things you've been dragging your feet on.

The unsuccessful person habitually thinks, "I know this task must be done, but it's hard, so I'll just put it off as long as I can." But the VICTORY PERSON makes a practice of thinking, "What I have to do may not be pleasant, but it must be done; therefore, I'll start on it right now so I can forget about it."

When faced with a decision, the victory-minded person doesn't put it off as long as he possibly can. He makes the decision or takes the action, and moves on to something else.

SUGGESTIONS FOR MAKING DECISIONS:

1. *Get All the Facts Available.*

2. *Study the Situation.* As thoroughly as you
    can, study the situation. Seek the counsel of
    God's Word. Ask advice of spiritual, mature
    people whom you respect. Don't place your
    faith in the words of unsuccessful, worldly,
    compromising individuals. One of the Bible
    principles of success is found in the first
    chapter of Psalms: "Blessed is the man that
    walketh not in the counsel of the ungodly
    . . ." (Psalm 1:1). Why listen to the voice of
    failure and allow it to influence your think-
    ing?

3. *Go Over Various Courses of Action in Your
    Mind.* Weigh out the advantages and disad-
    vantages of deciding either way. Think in
    terms of the future and eternity; not just the
    "sweet here and now." God gave us good
    sense and expects us to use it when we can.
    "He grants good sense to the godly — His
    saints" (Proverbs 2:7-8 TLB).

4. *Ask God for Special Wisdom.* God will gladly
    grant you special wisdom if you'll ask for it in
    faith. Ask God, then believe you are receiving
    the answer (James 1:5-8; Jeremiah 33:3).

5.   *Listen for God's Answer.* The answer may come through a Scripture, a sermon, a godly friend, a Christian magazine article, or some other Scriptural way, but you can be sure of this — IT WILL COME; GOD WILL ANSWER! Make sure you expect it. "Morning by morning, O Lord, you hear my voice; morning by morning I lay my requests before you and WAIT IN EXPECTATION" (Psalm 5:3 NIV).

6.   *Pick a Course of Action and Take It!* "Commit to the Lord whatever you do, and your plans will succeed" (Proverbs 16:3 NIV).

7.   *Never Worry About a Decision You Made Yesterday.* In my lifetime, I have faced many challenging decisions, but there is one particular case you might be interested in hearing about.

Our ministry was growing. The responsibilities were becoming greater, but I was still a full-time employee with the City Power Company. The ministry could not expand unless I was able to devote more time to it, yet there weren't enough funds or pledges to support a full-time minister and carry on the ministry activities too. What was I to do? Should I "take a chance?" Should I enter full-time ministry uncertain whether or not I'd be able to make it? Should I leave the security of a well-paying job and begin into something that has the possibility of flopping? What should I do? If I enter the ministry in a full-time capacity, it might mean selling everything I own to keep my family from starving. What path should I take?

My wife and I applied the seven principles for decision making. We got all the facts available, studied the situation, went over possible courses of action, prayed, waited for God's answer, picked a course of action and took it!

I submitted the written notice of resignation to the City Power Company and entered full-time service for the Lord. Since that time, there have been some minor struggles, but nothing that could compare with the joy of knowing you're in the perfect will of God. Never once did we worry about whether or not we had made the right decision. We made it, and couldn't change it anyway, so what would be the use of worrying about it?

OVERCOMING PROCRASTINATION

Overcoming procrastination and developing decisiveness requires courage. At times, you will be called upon to make bold moves into areas you are perhaps unfamiliar with. But God is with you. Jesus Christ is your Light of Life.

Don't allow the sin of procrastination to rob you of the success God desires you to experience. Don't put off until next week that which should have been done last week. Life is too short to permit a habit such as this to steal the victory that is rightfully ours in Christ.

> "As long as it is day, we must do the work of Him Who sent Me. Night is coming, when no man can work" (John 9:4 NIV).

> "Behold, *NOW* is the accepted time; behold, *NOW* is the day of salvation" (2 Corinthians 6:2).

IN QUICK REVIEW:

1. Don't wait until it's too late. Don't procrastinate.

2. True faith is *NOW*.

3. One of the chief qualities of effective leadership is DECISIVENESS.

4. The double-minded person can EXPECT FAILURE.

5. How to overcome procrastination: (a) Start RIGHT NOW (b) Make it a way of life to be decisive.

6. Seven Principles for decision making:

    (a) Get all the facts.

    (b) Study the situation.

(c) Go over in your mind various courses of action.

(d) Pray.

(e) Listen for God's answer.

(f) Pick a course of action and take it.

(g) Never lament over a decision you made yesterday.

YOUR SUCCESS PRINCIPLE FOR TODAY: DON'T PROCRASTINATE — LEARN TO MAKE DECISIONS!

CHAPTER THREE

YOUR SUCCESS PRINCIPLE FOR TODAY:

Get to Work!

TEXT: *"My Father is always at His work to this very day, and I, too, am working"* (John 5:17 NIV).

Did you know that God, the Father, is at work, even this very day? Did you know that Jesus, after ascending into Heaven, didn't just sit down to retire, relax, and take things easy? No sir! They are both working to this very day.

Jesus is working as the Great High Priest, Intercessor, Mediator, and Head of the Church (Hebrews 4:14, 7:25, 9:15, 1 Timothy 2:5, Ephesians 1:22). In addition, He is at work preparing a place in eternity for believers to live forever (John 14:2). No, the Lord didn't go on vacation after rising from the dead; He went into Heaven because He had a position to fulfill; a job to do.

Here is a success principle: Get to work! God has given YOU a position to fulfill; a job to do. In order to experience success in any endeavor, you must first begin. Start doing the task God has given you. Faith without action is dead. Faith which is not accompanied by works is not true faith at all; it's dead faith (James 2:26).

You have received the Lord's guidance. You have made the decision to quit procrastinating. Now, it's time to begin. It's time to put action to your faith and start planning, preparing, and working.

LAZINESS

There is a common tendency in the human race toward laziness. It's easier NOT TO learn something new than it is TO learn something new. It's more comfortable NOT TO work than it is TO work. Laziness is a sin that each of us must combat if we are to be victorious, successful Christians.

Jesus spoke about an unfruitful servant in Matthew 25. The real reason that the servant was not productive or successful, Jesus revealed, was because he was "slothful!" In other words, he was just plain L-A-Z-Y!

BROTHER SLOUCH

Brother Slouch couldn't understand why he was passed over for promotion so many times. He blamed it on the fact that "the boss doesn't like me.'' He also used the excuse: ''I'm just a slow learner and can't pick things up as quickly as others.'' Well, the truth of the matter is this: When he should have been reading technical manuals, Slouch was browsing through the national scandal sheets. When he should have been giving the boss a good eight-hour day, he was using the phone, making plans for the new house he was building, and conducting other personal business on company time. He was accomplishing in five hours that which should have been completed in one hour had he worked at it.

"Oh, I like to take my time and do a good job,'' said Brother Slouch. That would be fine if it were true. But it's not. The truth of the matter is that Slouch's workmanship was substandard. It was no better than the other's who were being five times more productive. Brother Slouch, instead of admitting his slothfulness, and renouncing it as sin, chose to make excuses for not being promoted — a tragic choice.

You can't humanly help a lazy man. He'll have an excuse for his failure every time you try to teach him Bible success principles.

"The slothful man saith, There is a lion in the way; a lion is in the streets'' (Proverbs 26:13).

Although neatly disguised, he's making an excuse for his laziness. Why doesn't he succeed? There is something ''in the way!'' In this instance it was a lion.

An excellent example of this type of excuse-making today is found in the fallacy "there just aren't any jobs available." This statement can be refuted on the precepts of God's Word and on the basis of personal experience. There *ARE* jobs available. Using the faith God has given you (Romans 12:3), you *CAN* secure employment . . . if you really want to work.

Usually, the lazy man goes unyielded to godly reason. You see, he knows it all! He is wise in his own conceits. The best thing to do for this poor individual is to pray for him, asking God to help him see the destructiveness of being lazy.

"The sluggard is wiser in his own conceit than seven men that can render a reason" (Proverbs 26:16).

Laziness breaks up relationships, disintegrates personalities, and causes untold family problems. Laziness will keep a person poor.

"Yet a little sleep, a little slumber, a little folding of the hands to sleep: So shall poverty come . . ." (Proverbs 24:33-34a).

MY WIFE'S EXPERIENCE

After my wife, Mary Jo, graduated from Bible College (this was before we married), she wanted to get a job at a bank. She prayed and believed that God would provide her with the employment and position she desired.

> ". . . What things soever ye *DESIRE,* when ye
> *PRAY, BELIEVE* that ye *RECEIVE* them, and
> ye shall have them" (Mark 11:24).

Putting action to her faith, she started filling
out employment application forms at various
banks she thought she'd like to work. With deter-
mination, she went from bank to bank, never letting go of God's promise: " . . . and ye SHALL
have them." In one week's time, she had the job
and the position she wanted. (Incidentally, it was at
the best paying bank in town!)

ACHIEVE!!

Man was placed here on Earth to achieve. We
were put here to work (Genesis 2:15). If we don't
work, we aren't fulfilling God's plan, thus, we can
expect failure and poverty to overtake our lives.

But God gives us a choice. He is no respector of
persons. We can choose to be diligent and become
leaders, achieving great things for God's glory. Or,
we can choose to be slothful (lazy), resulting in
bondage.

> "The hand of the diligent shall bear rule: but
> the slothful shall be under tribute (bondage)"
> (Proverbs 12:24).

THE ENEMY'S LIES

There is a multitude, however, of sincere, honest individuals who genuinely desire to be achievers in this life, but somehow the enemy has fed them a lie which they believed, consequently, their progress was stunted. Let's take a look at some of the devil's lies which keep people from pressing forward:

LIE NUMBER ONE: **"Just keep confessing it and** *someday* **it will come to pass.**

Someday you'll be a victorious Christian. *Someday* you'll be successful. *Someday* your "boat" will come in."

The Bible Laws of confession are powerful and 100% accurate. It *IS* extremely important that the words of our mouth line up with God's Word (Joshua 1:8). But it seems that whenever a truth is taught, somebody will come along, misinterpret, misuse, misapply, and carry it to an unscriptural extreme.

The enemy would love to have you doing nothing more than talking big.

"Someday our church will have 500 members!"

"Someday, in the future, I'm going to step out in faith on the call of God on my life."

"Someday I'm going to read the Bible all the way through."

"Someday, if I just keep confessing it, I know I'll be successful, and fruitful for God."

Talk all you want. Dream all you want. But if you don't START WORKING, you will most undoubtedly fail.

When I was just a kid growing up in Jackson, Michigan, I remember when my dad bought me one of those three-speed, skinny-tired bikes. Wow! Those skinny tires were really the "in" thing back then. All the "cool ones" had bikes with skinny tires. Well, I could have sat around all day long saying things like this:

"Someday I'm going to ride this bike."

"Someday I'm going to get that bike going in a forward direction and really go places!"

"Someday I'll become a skilled bike rider."

But, if I hadn't hopped on that bike and STARTED, I never would have gotten anywhere. Do you see what I am saying?

"Faith without *ACTION* is dead" (James 2:26 TEV).

After Paul, the apostle, got saved and filled with the Holy Spirit, the Bible declares, "AT ONCE he began to preach in the synagogues that Jesus is the Son of God" (Acts 9:20 NIV). He didn't sit around talking about how at some unspecified time in the future he would begin to preach about Jesus. No, he took positive action at once.

You can take action NOW! Start asking God for His guidance. Start planning. Start setting goals. And most importantly, take that first step. A trip of a hundred miles begins with the first step. Your journey to success and achievement begins when you take the first step.

As you travel, you'll find God beginning to supply you with the necessary tools to make your destination reachable. He will provide you with finances, if needed. He will send the right people your way who will want to help you attain your God-given goals. He'll communicate bigger ideas to you and increase your vision — but you must take that first step and START!

Begin moving forward, and by all means, maintain a good, solid Bible confession. But add to your confession ACTION. That's real faith.

LIE NUMBER TWO: **"There will be nothing but problems. It won't be worth the time you spend on it."**

This is another lie that keeps people paralyzed; they fear all the problems that may occur in new ventures. Recently I read about a lady who never got married because she was worried about all the problems that might befall the new relationship. When she died, here's what they engraved as an epitaph on her tombstone:

"Here lies the bones of Miss Betsy Jones.
"She wanted no problems, she wanted no terrors;
"She lived an old maid, and died an old maid,
"No runs, no hits, no errors!"

Certainly there will be *some* problems in every new venture the Lord gives you. But these problems weren't meant to be "killers"; they were intended to help you grow and mature in your faith. Don't let the thought of problems hold you back from beginning.

Jesus didn't tell us to sit still just because of a few problems, or what you might call "mountains." He didn't tell us to wait until all the mountains are gone before we begin. He told us that if we would exercise our faith, we could move those mountains! (Matthew 17:20)

Believe it or not, problems can be exciting opportunities for our faith to grow. In a previous chapter, we mentioned that faith needs two things in order to grow: (1) the Word of God (2) exercise. Problems give us the opportunity to exercise our faith. (A word of caution: Don't try to manufacture your own problems. We are not talking about self-induced troubles. We are referring to the problems that seem to find their way into every God-called project.)

The enemy would love nothing more than to burden us down with thoughts about all the problems. He wants to hinder our progress. Sadly

enough, untold thousands of undiscerning individuals have fallen into this trap. Because his
nature is to lie (John 8:44), the devil grossly exag-
gerates every problem. The "mountains" are never
as big or bad as he says they will be.

For example, have you ever thought about
going next door to let your new neighbors know
about Jesus Christ? The devil probably said to you,
"You better not. They'll kick you out of their
house. They'll get mad and you will have lost a
potentially good friend. Maybe they're satanists
and will decide to use YOU as a sacrifice!" Oh, the
devil gets bold!

Or how about the time you felt called into the
ministry? The enemy was right there to show you
all the problems ahead. "You won't have anymore
health insurance like you have at your present occupation. You'll have a heart attack just as soon as
you turn in your resignation. Your ministry will fail
within thirty days. What if you have another child?
How will you be able to support your family?"

When problems start coming to your mind, just
remember this: Problems are only mountains. And
the person of faith knows that mountains *CAN* be
moved!

LIE NUMBER THREE: **"Other people sure won't
like that! You'll be the most unpopular person in
the school (or office, or factory, or wherever you
are)."**

Whenever you are walking in the will of God and your life is being directed by the Holy Spirit, you can most certainly expect some criticism and opposition. But some people are so afraid of persecution, they never move ahead at all. They're so afraid of ruining their reputation, they end up developing *no* reputation. When we become more concerned about what other people think instead of what God thinks, we are headed for trouble!

In the Bible we are told of those who were more concerned about what *people* thought than they were about what *God* thought. They were real losers!

"For they loved the praise of men more than the praise of God" (John 12:43).

Pilate had Jesus crucified, NOT because he felt that Jesus was guilty, but because he was afraid of what people would think if he didn't. Pilate was a loser! He was stuck in a self-imposed bondage of "what-will-other-people-think?" This is a common and destructive failure-producing spiritual prison (John 19:12-16).

BROTHER JITTER

Brother Jitter had the call of God to preach the Gospel. He graduated from a renowned Bible School but wouldn't go before the district council to get his license to preach because he was afraid they wouldn't approve him. He was bound by the thought "what-will-they-think?"

All sorts of thoughts crossed Brother Jitter's mind — "Maybe my clothes are too fashionable and they'll think I'm a hippie!" So he went out and purchased a more conservative suit. Then the thought came to him, "They'll probably think I'm a phoney because I'm too young to wear this style." His mind was paralyzed.

If it wasn't one thing it was another (pardon me for using this old cliche!) Brother Jitter ended up working as a gas station attendant all his life because he was too concerned about "what-will-other-people-think?" Oh yes, he was a Christian. But he certainly missed out on God's best for his life.

Would you like to become less self-conscious and be released from the bondage that kept Brother Jitter from succeeding in life? Then simply become more Jesus-conscious. The Bible gives us a key in Hebrews 12:2 —

"Looking unto Jesus the author and finisher of our faith. . . ."

We must deliberately, as an act of our will, fix our eyes, not on ourselves, but on Jesus. Don't concentrate on your*self*, or your critics — concentrate on Jesus. Study His Life. See how He handled various situations and YOU handle them the same way. That's one way we "look unto Jesus."

Always remember this fact: The bigger you grow and the farther you go, the more critics you will have. They will criticize you if you are right. They will criticize you if you are wrong. Some people are just watching you, waiting to criticize and accuse.

> "And the scribes and Pharisees watched him, whether he would heal on the sabbath day; that they might find an accusation against him" (Luke 6:7).

Just be yourself! God made you unique. You are one of a kind. There is no other person on earth quite like you. Therefore, be genuine, honest and original. God threw away the blueprint when He made you. Don't try to "be somebody" by conforming to the approval of others. Simply allow the Holy Spirit to do *His* conforming work in your life (2 Corinthians 3:18). Stay close to Jesus. Be relaxed and at ease around others and don't be trapped by the bondage of "what-will-others-think?"

Sure, other people will disapprove of some of the things you do, but you must do what you know is right. In the long run, people will respect you for standing up for what you believe is right. Satan loves to see Christians become "wishy-washy" compromisers. You do what is right — do what God wants you to, and quit worrying about what other people will think!

> "The fear of man bringeth a snare: but whoso putteth his trust in the Lord shall be safe" (Proverbs 29:25).

LIE NUMBER FOUR — "You are now too old!"

Not long ago I was having a conversation with a 55-year-old man who had worked in the same place for the past thirty years. I'll call him Bob Lifer. Bob disliked his job immensely but wouldn't change.

"Well, Dave," he replied, "I'm 55 now. I'm getting old and it's too late for me to change jobs now. I sure would have enjoyed a career, but you know how it is. I'll be able to retire in a few years and I might as well just finish up right here. If I were young again, I would do it all differently though."

Bob was convinced that he was too old to "conquer new territories." He believed the same lie the enemy uses on multiplied thousands of people every day — "You're too old!" or "It's too late now!"

The Psalmist made an interesting observation —

"The length of our days is seventy years — or eighty if we have the strength . . ." (Psalm 90:10 NIV).

The normal human being is perfectly capable of being productive all the way up to, and often beyond seventy years of age; some even up to and beyond eighty.

"They (the righteous) will still bear fruit in old age, they will stay fresh and green . . ." (Psalm 92:14 NIV).

In the Bible we are told that Abraham, the father of all who have faith in Jesus, lived a long fruitful life.

"Then Abraham . . . died in a GOOD OLD AGE, an old man, and FULL OF YEARS" (Genesis 25:8).

Oftentimes people worry that they will be sick and crippled in their old age and unable to prosper and be fruitful. Medical science has recently discovered that worry is one of the very things that contribute to much of the sickness and disease in old age. Quit worrying! You're not getting older; you have eternity ahead of you.

MOSES

Moses was one hundred and twenty years old when he died, yet his eyesight was perfect and he was as strong as a young man (Deuteronomy 34:7).

CALEB

Caleb was 85 years old and still as strong as he was when he was 45! (Joshua 14:10-11) He was still powerful and vigorous — and he could still fight a good fight!

If you are now 60 years old, and are like Caleb, you have at least 25 fruitful years remaining. Much can be accomplished in 25 years. I know of a prominent evangelist who was just a "kid preacher" 20 years ago. Today the Lord has used him to affect the hearts and lives of individuals all over the face of the earth. Great achievements can be made in 20 or 25 years for the victory-minded person who is in tune with God's Spirit and refuses to be defeated.

Quit listening to the enemy. You're not too old to be successful. Don't let age stop you! Remember my bike with the skinny tires? Well I learned something about bikes from that. If you quit peddling, you will slowly come to a halt. It's extremely difficult to balance a bike while it's standing still. The same is true in life. We must keep peddling forward, no matter how young or how old we are.

> "Joshua was now an old man. You are growing old, the Lord said to him, and there are STILL MANY NATIONS TO BE CONQUERED!" (Joshua 13:1 TLB).

LIE NUMBER FIVE — "You haven't got enough education."

It's not wrong to have a formal education. St. Paul had one. But neither is it wrong NOT to have a formal training background. Some of the apostles were classified as ignorant and unlearned men (Acts 4:13). Uneducated by a structural system, these men turned the world "upside down." (Or should we say "rightside up?")

A highly successful pastor in a Midwestern city has no formal Bible Training, yet week after week people flock to church to sit under his ministry. Although not formally educated, God has given him the ability to make Jesus real to the people, and to make the Word of God come alive. People leave rejoicing after hearing the Word. So you see, the secret of success is not merely having a formal education — but Satan will tell you that it is.

LEE BRAXTON

Lee Braxton had a sixth grade education. After becoming a mechanic, he realized he had reached the top of the ladder; he had risen as far as he could. Soon, a godly dissatisfaction developed in Lee's heart and he began to pray for guidance from God. (You will find that men of real character will always ask for God's guidance in their lives.)

Lee read an inspirational book and began to believe that God is always a good God! He came to understand that there was a power working within himself to accomplish the impossible regardless of how little education he had (Ephesians 3:20).

Not long after reading that book, Lee organized and became the president of the First National Bank of Whiteville. Subsequently he became engaged in many successful business enterprises and was later elected as mayor of the city.

At the age of 44, Lee Braxton sold his businesses. Why did he sell out? To retire? To relax in the Florida sunshine for the rest of his life? To just lay down, roll up and die? Absolutely not! Today Lee Braxton is being tremendously used of God in helping one of the nation's leading evangelists. He is devoting his entire efforts to the ministry free of charge . . . and enjoying every minute of it!

God is no respector of persons. What He has done for others, He'll do for you — if you'll give Him a chance. As Stuart Hamlin so adequately said —

> "It is no secret, what God can do,
> What He's done for others —
> He'll do for you!"

Don't be disabled by the lie that says you can't make it without a great deal of education. You can be successful — just like Lee Braxton and others who have experienced high-level success with little or no formal training. Look at all you have going for you as a Christian. You have access to Wisdom from Above (James 1:5-8), the power of God is within you (Ephesians 3:20), and God is *for* you, not against you (Psalm 118:6). No education is no excuse. Don't tolerate this lie of your enemy.

LIE NUMBER SIX — "You've failed so much in the past, you're bound to fail again."

To be successful and victorious, we must learn to identify with Christ, not our past failures. Paul said it this way:

". . . Forgetting those things which are behind, and reaching forth unto those things which are before" (Philippians 3:13).

How do we forget those negative things of the past? Here's how: By reaching forth; by pushing in a forward direction. By moving ahead.

"Remember ye not the former things, neither consider the things of old. Behold, I WILL DO A NEW THING . . ." (Isaiah 43:18-19).

JOHN JILT

John Jilt owned a business at one time. It failed. Instead of seeking direction from God on how to gain capital to start again, he became bitter and went to work in an old dingy factory. He says that he'll never try again. Little does he realize that he's operating on an automatic failure system by giving up.

Let me explain. God has a plan for success that is guaranteed never to fail. It's called L-O-V-E.

"Love never fails . . ." (1 Corinthians 13:8 NIV).

One of the qualities of this plan for success is perseverance (1 Corinthians 13:7). That is the ability to get back up and take another swing regardless of how many times in the past you have struck out. Jesus spoke much about this quality of perseverance, especially in the area of prayer (Luke 18:1-8).

To achieve success, we must forget those past failures and begin to "reach forth" for that home run! Many people have quit just before they would have hit that grand slam they were pressing for.

BABE RUTH

At one time, Babe Ruth held the world's record for the most STRIKE OUTS! You didn't know that, did you? Well, he did! But he kept on swinging. He forgot about his failures, pushed on toward victory, and received the world's record for the most home runs. His secret: he kept swinging.

Sure, you've had failures in the past; you've "blown it." So have I and so has everybody else in the human race. But thank God, we can go to Him and know that Jesus Christ is right there, ready and willing to pull us back up to the triumphant life — we need only to "reach forth."

"The Lord is on my side; I will not fear . . ." (Psalm 118:6).

You can't fail when you realize that the Lord is on your side. He's not against you — He's for you! In your walk through life, there may be temporary set backs, but no permanent failures if Jesus Christ is your Lord. So quit viewing those little defeats as enormous failures. Reach forth to those things which are ahead. Just because you stumbled in the past doesn't necessarily mean you'll fail in the future.

> "Forget the former things: DO NOT DWELL ON THE PAST. . . ." (Isaiah 43:18-19 NIV).

> ". . . If any man be in Christ, he is a new creature: old things are passed away; behold, all things are become new" (2 Corinthians 5:17).

MORE SATANIC LIES

The enemy would love to render you ineffective and unproductive. One of the first Bible commands God gave to man was to "BE FRUITFUL!" By being fruitful and productive, we bring glory to God (John 15:8). Satan doesn't want God to get any glory at all, so he seeks to prevent us from achieving and being successful in whatever God has called us to do whether it's being a housewife, a doctor, a minister, a teacher, a policeman — whatever.

We have touched on some of the enemy's biggest lies designed to hold us back. There are others. Here are a few of them:

THE ENEMY SAYS:

*"You're too young!"

THE BIBLE SAYS:

"Let no man despise thy youth" (1 Timothy 4:12)

" . . . Your *sons* and your *daughters* shall prophesy" (Acts 2:17)

*"You're giving up all your security."

"For when they say peace and security, then destruction will come . . ." (1 Thessalonians 5:3a Paraphrased)

*"Wait until conditions are more perfect."

"If you wait for perfect conditions, you will never get anything done" (Ecclesiastes 11:4 TLB).

Too many times we have let the enemy convince us that we can't do something that God says we can. God says we can move mountains with faith. With faith, we can accomplish the impossible. One of the most important keys is this: GET STARTED! Begin working and planning and preparing — BEGIN NOW.

Where will you be five years from now if you don't begin? Don't try to balance your "bike" standing still — start pedaling!

God is the most successful Person there is. Read His book. He never failed. We should follow His example and get to work on accomplishing His objectives in our lives.

Jesus said, "My Father is ALWAYS at His work to this very day, and I too am working" (John 5:17 NIV).

"Do not despise this small beginning, for the eyes of the Lord rejoice to see the work begin . . ." (Zechariah 4:10 TLB).

Don't let the enemy trap you with lies and excuses. Get busy. Let the work begin and the eyes of the Lord will rejoice!

IN QUICK REVIEW:

1. Laziness is a sin that each person must combat if he is to be successful.

2. Man was placed on earth to achieve; thereby bringing glory to God.

3. Some of the devil's lies:

   (a) "Someday you'll be successful if you keep confessing it."

   (b) "Success isn't worth the time you spend achieving it."

   (c) "You'll be very unpopular if you start achieving for God."

   (d) "You're just too old to start now."

   (e) "You haven't got enough education."

   (f) "You're bound to fail — you've failed so much in the past."

   (g) "You're too young."

   (h) "You'll be giving up all your security. Don't take the chance."

   (i) "It would be better to wait for more perfect conditions."

4.   Do not despise the day of small beginnings.

5.   Put joy into the eyes of God — let the work begin!

CHAPTER FOUR

YOUR SUCCESS PRINCIPLE
FOR TODAY:

Watch That Bragging!

TEXT: *"Not every one that saith unto me, Lord, Lord, shall enter into the kingdom of heaven; but he that doeth the will of my Father which is in heaven. Many will say to me in that day, Lord, Lord, have we not prophesied in thy name? and in thy name have cast out devils? and in thy name done many wonderful works? And then will I profess unto them, I never knew you: depart from me, ye that work iniquity"* (Matthew 7:21-23).

It sounds to me like these fellows were trying to get into heaven by bragging about what THEY had done instead of what CHRIST had done.

Have you ever met up with somebody who knew everything about everything and whatever anybody else has ever done, he has done it better? Well, what did you think? Were you impressed? The dictionary has a name for a person like that — braggart! That is a person who is given to boring, empty boasting . . . usually about himself.

The person who does all the bragging and the person who is remarkably successful are rarely the same person. When an individual continually boasts about *him*self and *his* accomplishments, you can be sure of this: others will begin to close their ears to him. Even if the poor fellow does have some good things to say, they will be unfruitful because of his boastful attitude. Bragging and victory just don't go together.

Jesus didn't come bragging about Himself. He never bragged about His ministry either. You never heard Jesus saying things like this: "Yes, folks, here I am, the Son of God! Come to my rallies and witness the phenomenal miracles I am performing on the sick. Yes, folks, step right this way and watch people crowd around me as I speak these words of wisdom from above!" No, Jesus didn't have to brag on Himself or His ministry. The "proof was in the pudding" so to speak. In other words, the miracles spoke for themselves as well as did the teaching.

My wife and I met an interesting fellow while attending a district council dinner and convention recently. He was a traveling evangelist who was boasting about his ministry. "Hundreds — slain in the Spirit . . . healings and creative miracles! Yes, even cult members were receiving the Holy Ghost and fallin' out under the power!" My wife and I looked at each other and sort of smiled. We could tell the young man was sincere in his heart, but was perhaps a bit exaggerative in his speaking. Certainly he meant well, but his testimony was rendered invalid because of the boastful way he handled himself.

No, it's not wrong to speak and to testify of the wonderful things God is doing. But we must be careful to do it in a way that doesn't sound as though we are bragging on ourselves. When we brag on or commend ourselves, we are beginning to operate on another automatic failure system.

> "But let him who boasts boast in the Lord. For it is NOT the man who commends himself who is approved, but the man whom the Lord commends" (2 Corinthians 10:17, 18 NIV).

EXAMPLE OF SPIRITUAL BOASTING

Here's an example of spiritual boasting: "You should have seen *ME* witnessing to that guy the other day. *I* led him right to the foot of the cross through *MY* amazing power of *PERSONAL* persuasion!" You see, this fellow was actually praising himself in a rather subtle way.

> "Let another praise you, and not your own mouth; someone else, and not your own lips" (Proverbs 27:2 NIV).

DON'T DRIVE AWAY YOUR TEAM
BY BOASTING

No person in history has ever been highly successful all by himself. Victory-minded people know that it takes a team in order to achieve eminent, high-level success. Jesus appointed a team. Each had their specific duties and functions as part of that team. Today God still uses team effort to accomplish His purposes in the earth (1 Corinthians 12).

Success depends largely on the support of other people. Don't misunderstand, we *must* depend upon God as our Sustaining Source, but at the same time remembering that God uses *people* to support and accomplish His objectives in our lives. Without other people's backing, we will never be greatly successful.

Nehemiah couldn't have rebuilt the Jerusalem wall without the support of people (Nehemiah 2:17-18; 4:6).

David could not have won so many battles without building a great team first (1 Chronicles 12:1-14).

Solomon could not have constructed that monumental, mammoth-sized temple without the help and cooperation of others (1 Chronicles 2-6).

The Prophet Daniel was a highly successful man in his day. Notice: he requested the appointment of qualified assistants (team members). (See Daniel 2:49.)

Jesus appointed a crew — a team, in order that He might broaden His earthly ministry (Mark 3:13-19).

The Early Church elected qualified men to handle certain affairs that the apostles had not the time for (Acts 6:1-7).

Teamwork has always been a part of God's plan for our success. Moses appointed a team 1400 years before Christ was born (Exodus 18:17-26). The Levites in the Old Testament worked together as a team. Each clan had its own special set of responsibilities. (See Numbers, chapter three.)

People want to help you succeed! People need to feel like a part of the team; they need to feel as though they belong. God made us that way so that we would need and help each other (Romans 15:1).

But a man will drive people away from his team if he is continually boasting about himself. It makes people feel as though they are unimportant, unneeded. Consequently, they leave and join up with some other cooperative effort and the braggart is left alone to struggle in his failure.

AN ILLUSTRATION

I was sitting in church one Sunday night when the song leader began to commend the pastor on his magnificent sermons and his accomplishments around the community. The pastor stepped up into the pulpit and didn't take an ounce of the credit for his achievements! He said, "It's not really because of me or my abilities. You see, every Saturday evening people come here to pray for me, the congregation, and others in the community. I'm sort of like a milkman. He delivers the milk, but he doesn't produce it."

That reply made people *want* to stand behind him. He gave God the glory and handed some of the credit to his team members too! Today this pastor is considered by many to be the top spiritual leader in the district. People look up to him. Other pastors seek his advice and help. He is a successful, fruitful man of God.

> ". . . They refreshed my spirit and yours also. Such men deserve recognition" (1 Corinthians 16:18 NIV).

One of the keys of effective leadership is to share the credits and honors with your staff and associates. Don't be a boring boaster and take all the honor for yourself. That's a good way to F-A-I-L!

> "A man's pride brings him low, but a man of lowly spirit gains honor" (Proverbs 29:23 NIV).

> "Do you see a man wise in his own eyes? There is more hope for a fool than for him" (Proverbs 26:12 NIV).

If you want to lose the support of other people and make them shun you, here is the way to do it: Brag about yourself! Talk incessantly about yourself and your so-called achievements. Never take the time to recognize nor give credit to God or to other people. After all, you are so much "more important than they are!"

THE STORY OF GLENN GLORYHOG AND HARRY HONORSHARE

Glenn Gloryhog was the senior man on the maintenance crew at a local factory. He was next in line to be promoted to the position of maintenance foreman. In fact, he was acting as the assistant foreman in preparation for assuming the duties of his upcoming advancement. Glenn was certainly an experienced mechanic, but was lacking in one area of leadership which cost him his chance of climbing up a rung on the management ladder.

Every opportunity Glenn would visit the plant manager's office to make his "reports." While he was in there, he would boast about all the work *HE* was getting out of *HIS* men. He conveyed the attitude, "I don't know how this plant would survive without *ME!*" The poor men. They were doing all the work, and it appeared as though Glenn was taking all the credit.

Meanwhile, Harry Honorshare was working as a mechanic's leader. Harry had less seniority than

Glenn, and never considered being promoted to the position of plant maintenance foreman, but had a powerful leadership characteristic that Glenn never developed. Whenever his work crew did a good job, he would thank them and let them know how much he appreciated their cooperation and outstanding workmanship. Whenever the plant manager would take notice of the work and compliment it, Harry would always say, "Well, it couldn't have been done without my crew. They are the ones that really deserve the credit."

One day Harry received a letter from the main office asking him if he'd consider accepting the responsibilities of plant maintenance foreman. Glenn was not promoted.

One thing Glenn had not learned is this: You'll never elevate yourself in people's eyes or in God's eyes by boasting about yourself. You'll never rise to a position of honor by putting others down.

". . . Humility comes *before* honor" (Proverbs 15:33 NIV).

"For everyone who exalts himself will be humbled, and he who humbles himself will be exalted" (Luke 18:14 NIV).

"It is not good to eat too much honey, nor is it honorable to seek one's own honor" (Proverbs 25:27 NIV).

The victory-minded person does not think more highly of himself than he ought, but thinks soberly.

In other words, he judges himself with an accurate judgement (Romans 12:3). It's easy for a person to overrate his importance and begin to boast in himself. Equally as true, it's common for a person to underrate himself and habitually speak and think negatively about himself and his calling in life. Both are bad extremes. The true victory-minded person is a well-balanced, well-adjusted Christian who realizes that in himself, he is but dust, but in Christ he is the salt of the earth; the light of the world! (Matthew 5:13, 14).

HOW TO KEEP FROM BOASTING

But how do we keep from boasting? There just seems to be "something" in us human beings that wants to brag a little bit about ourselves. How do we prevent this automatic failure system from actuating?

Henry Ford told us of a plan that will keep us from boasting about our petty accomplishments. He said, "Make your program so long and so difficult, that when people praise you for what you have accomplished, it will seem as nothing in comparison with what you are aiming to do." In other words, keep setting new and higher goals. You'll be so busy moving forward, you won't have time to boast about your small achievements of the past.

The successful person looks for things to boast about in other people. The *self*ish person looks for things to boast about in himself. The successful person honors others above himself (Romans 12:10). The *self*ish person honors himself above others. To illustrate how the victory-minded Christian looks for things to boast about in others, look at St. Paul. He boasted to the Macedonians about the Corinthian's eagerness to help Christians in other parts of the world. (See 2 Corinthians 9:2.) And Paul certainly was successful at his calling in life.

The successful person says much to encourage and strengthen other people. (See Acts 15:32.) The self-seeking person doesn't have the time to encourage others because he is too busy thinking and talking about himself! Little does the braggart realize that boasting is nothing more than a deep form of selfishness and here's what selfishness will do for a person:

1. Selfishness will keep you from experiencing a close walk with Jesus Christ.

2. Selfishness will drive people away from you.

3. Selfishness will keep you alone.

4. Selfishness will tear down relationships.

5. Selfishness will disintegrate your personality.

6.   Selfishness will destroy your life.

Love is not self-seeking (1 Corinthians 13:5) and love never fails (1 Corinthians 13:8). If a person is selfish, he is not abiding in love. Therefore, he is operating on an unconscious, self-actuated losing game of failure. Love never fails but selfishness always fails.

Here are a few more suggestions on how to prevent bragging on yourself:

1.   Develop an honest appreciation for God and for others.

2.   Take time to think about God and others. This takes your mind off yourself. Take the time to think about other's feelings, their problems, their desires, their needs.

3.   Treat others like they are important! People won't put up with being treated like numbers or machines for very long. Jesus treated people like they were really important — because they were! They were important enough for Him to die for. (So are you and I!)

Jesus didn't come bragging and boasting about Himself. He could have. After all, He was God Incarnate; the Creator of the universe. But He came, not seeking His own glory, but the glory of the Heavenly Father.

Cheryl Prewitt, Miss America 1980, publicly declared that she owes God all the credit for her beauty crown. Truly beautiful people, victorious people will always have a humble way of giving God the glory for any and all success in their lives.

Remember — the VICTORY PERSON is not a braggart!

> "In God we boast all the day long, and praise Thy name forever" (Psalm 44:8).

IN QUICK REVIEW:

1. *DO* boast in the Lord (Psalm 44:8; 34:2).

2. *DO* boast in others (2 Corinthians 9:2, 3).

3. *DON'T* boast in yourself (Romans 1:30, 2 Timothy 3:2, Psalm 10:3).

(Remember: Boasting in yourself is an automatic failure system!)

CHAPTER FIVE

YOUR SUCCESS PRINCIPLE
FOR TODAY:

Finish What You Begin!

TEXT: *"My food is to do the will of Him Who sent Me and to FINISH HIS WORK"* (John 4:34 NIV).

God has a specific work for each of us to accomplish. When we discover what that work is, and begin to aim our talents and efforts in that direction, we will discover a new dimension of adventure, excitement, and contentment in our lives like we've never experienced before.

When we find what our purpose and calling in life is, it is important to persist in that direction. Some people start doing what God wants them to, but for some reason, perhaps the trials, they fail to follow through. Jesus said His food was not only to *DO* the will of the Father, but to FINISH THAT WORK. Herein is a great principle for success: Follow through, persist, persevere, hang in there!

Stop and think for a moment. How many projects have you known of that started out well, but slowly fizzled out? How many times have you begun to act on a great idea from God, but for some reason failed to persevere and accomplish your goals? Lack of perseverance is a common hindrance to the success of any project or program we start for the Lord.

BROTHER SHIFTY

Brother Shifty always felt "called" to work with young people. He always talked about how someday he was going to be a real leader of today's youth. One day the opportunity was presented to him to work as the youth director of the junior church. With great enthusiasm he accepted the offer and immediately had visions of a great youth revival. He began creating plans for youth projects and started putting them into effect. There was only one problem. Every time a trial or problem came to an implemented project or plan, Shifty would call it "quits" and begin to push in another direction. He failed to learn one of the most important principles of success: FINISH WHAT GOD GUIDES YOU TO BEGIN! FOLLOW THROUGH. BE PERSISTENT — like Jesus was.

Solomon said, "Finishing is better than starting" (Ecclesiastes 7:8 TLB). Every time we step out in faith on God's Word or God's call, there will always be some problems. It's a universal law — if there are no trials at all, the chances are, it's not a worthwhile project.

When trials come (and they will come) don't quit. Jesus didn't quit. He persisted in a forward direction, even in the midst of His greatest challenges. Don't you give up either! FINISH THE WORK!

JESUS DIDN'T GIVE UP

Jesus had trials and problems in His ministry. He was with His disciples for three and one half years teaching them, ministering to them, and telling them secrets about the Kingdom of God, yet they were still dull in their understanding of who He was and what He was here for. At this point it would have been easy for Jesus to look at the situation and say, "Oh, forget it! I came to save these people and look . . . after all this time my disciples still don't understand my mission, the religious leaders are against me, and the crowds are beginning to die down. What's the use? I'm calling it quits!"

No, no, no! Jesus did no such thing. He didn't quit. Even when adversity stared Him right in the face, He kept moving forward. When things began to look grim, when it seemed as though everything He did came to naught, when everyone was leaving Him, and everything appeared to be going wrong, HE STILL DIDN'T QUIT!

One of the last things Jesus said while on the cross was, "It is finished." He finished the work He started.

WAS JESUS SUCCESSFUL?

Let me ask you a question. Was Jesus successful? Let's take a look and see. Please note the fact that the Name of Jesus Christ is the best known Name in the entire world. There are people on every continent on the face of the earth that know Him personally. Our calendars are dated from His birth. Jesus was (and still is) the most successful leader of all times. What other leader has governed men for hundreds of years? What other leader ever rose from the dead? What other leader has been directing and influencing the lives of multiplied millions for several centuries? No other but Jesus Christ! Now I would say that is success!

Jesus finished the work He was sent to do. He finished the plan of salvation. He destroyed the works of the enemy at Calvary (1 John 3:8). He was the most successful Leader that ever lived, and He gave us this success principle: FINISH FOR GOD WHAT YOU BEGIN FOR GOD.

MY EXPERIENCE

The first time I had ever preached in a large church, I felt like a big F-A-I-L-U-R-E. I was so nervous, I could hardly speak. Everything seemed to go wrong. My voice was squeaky and shaky, the delivery of the message left much to be desired, and to top it all off, I forgot my ministry manners and slouched up against the pulpit while I was speaking! Oh, you could not believe how utterly horrible I felt afterwards. To me, it was as if my whole career was crumbling. I had failed.

When my wife and I returned home after church that evening, I told her, "I'm all done! I'm never preachin' again. In fact, I'm never going to even set foot in that church again. I failed you, I failed Pastor Snook (he was the pastor who invited me to speak), I failed that congregation, and worst of all, I failed God!" (I didn't realize it then, but now I can see that I was beginning to function on a self-actuated failure system called "LACK-OF-PERSISTENCE").

Well, I thank God for a great wife and a wonderful pastor who encouraged me to stick to it; to do what God had called me to do. So I did (stick with it), and have been ever since.

God wants us to finish what He calls us to begin. Thousands of people start out well, but when they run into trouble, they fall by the wayside. If we are to experience any degree of success at all, we must stick with it. We must develop persistence, perseverance, tenacity, STICK-TO-IT-IVENESS!

BLIND BARTIMAEUS

When Bartimaeus came to ask Jesus for the healing of his eyes, people told him to shut up. But instead of shutting up, he shouted all the louder. As a result of his persistent faith, he received the healing he was asking for; he gained his eyesight. He was persistent and it brought about success for this blind beggar (Mark 10:46-53).

When the devil tells you to quit, to give up, to throw in the towel, that's the time to turn on the "superheaters," like Bartimaeus, and go full speed ahead.

The winning attitude of persistence is illustrated in the words of Micah, the prophet:

". . . Though I fall, I will rise again" (Micah 7:8 TLB).

And King Solomon said it this way:

"For though a righteous man falls seven times, he rises again" (Proverbs 24:16 NIV).

Sure, there will be times when you will begin to wonder if God really did call you to begin the venture. It's common to wonder things like this. You will have thoughts like these:

"Am I really in the will of God?"

"Perhaps I've made so many mistakes, God has given up on me!"

"Maybe I failed to discern the Lord's guidance and wasn't really led of Him to begin this thing."

It's a common tactic of the enemy to tell you that you are out of God's will and something terrible will soon happen to you. He'll try to make you think that God will "zap you dead" if you don't quit your silly project. Listen — God is perfectly capable of letting you know when the time to stop is and when the time to move is. If you love Jesus and are staying in the Word and in prayer, He can let you know when to stop and when to start. Quit worrying about it! You just "hold fast . . ." and "press on toward your challenging goals." Don't allow a minor problem, a little defeat, a bit of confusion, or a nugget of criticism stop you from moving ahead. Press on until you finish.

American humorist, Josh Billings, put this principle into a humorous expression:

> "Consider the postage stamp, my son. It secures success through its ability to STICK TO ONE THING until it gets there."

THE MINISTRY OF JESUS

When Jesus was being opposed and threatened by King Herod and the Pharisees, He didn't stop His ministry. His reply to their threats was essentially this: "I'll keep right on doing what I came to do until the work is finished. I'll keep right on casting out devils and healing the sick and working miracles" (Luke 13:31-33). Jesus was determined to FINISH the work His Father had sent Him to do.

The reason many people fail today is they haven't made the quality decision to stick with it. They say, "I'll try it for a while and see if it works out." It never will work out that way. You see, that is *not* a quality decision; that's a double-minded person. And the Bible clearly declares that a double-minded person can expect *NOTHING* from the Lord (James 1:5-8). We must make the decision to persevere regardless of all enemy opposition.

Men and women who totally commit themselves to FINISHING the work God has given them to do will find themselves becoming increasingly successful as the days go by. You can't force a person to quit when he has determined in his heart and resolved in his mind to stick with it to the finish.

Here are some examples of the difference between success-bound people and failure-bound people:

Situation:	Failure-Bound:	Success-Bound:
1. Salvation	"I'm going to try it for a while, perhaps a few weeks, and just see if things really do get better."	"In the Name of Jesus, I am now a child of God and with His grace and help I'll *never* turn back to my old life — no matter what!"
2. Baptism in Holy Spirit	"I'll just sit here and see if anything really happens. If it doesn't, I'll know God doesn't want me to have it."	"I'll study the Scriptures to build my faith, I'll pray, and praise God, I'm going to receive this experience. It's promised, it's mine, and in Jesus' Name I'm going to have it!"

3. Call of God	"I'm going to try to be a preacher. Maybe God will open some doors and if I preach good, maybe I can become an evangelist. But if things don't work out, I can always get my old job back at the factory."	"God has called me to the ministry. I'll study, pray, meditate upon God's Word, and I will preach the Gospel. No matter what happens, I'll *NEVER* go back to secular employment unless specifically directed to do so by God Himself."
4. Divine Healing	"God will heal me someday if it's His will. If I don't get healed in tomorrow's service, I'll know that God will somehow be getting glory out of my sickness."	"Praise God! The Word says that Jesus bore my sicknesses and carried my diseases — that means I don't have to. God is willing to heal me, I claim it, confess it, believe it, and receive it by faith right now!"
5. God's Financial Plan	"Well, I'll try it for two weeks; I'll give God 10% of my earnings for two weeks, and if I don't start getting prosperous immediately, I'll know that it doesn't really work."	"With God's help, I'm going to give tithes and offerings to His work. I choose to make giving a way of life simply because the Bible tells me to. I will not compromise on this matter under ANY circumstances. I will persist in giving to God and believe He will reward me accordingly."

FINISH WHAT YOU START

God is interested in us FINISHING what He tells us to start. The beauty of it is this: God will help us to complete our task if we will but do our part and NEVER GIVE UP. The result is success . . . and who doesn't want to be successful for God?

When we complete the work God has given us, our lives will bring glory to our Heavenly Father (John 17:4). Jesus brought glory to the Father by *finishing* the work He was sent to do.

> "I have glorified Thee on the earth; I have fin-
> ished the work which Thou gavest Me to do"
> (Jesus praying to the Father, John 17:4).

The Bible is full of examples of men and women
of faith who FINISHED the task God gave them to
begin. They accomplished their purpose in spite of
the trials, the tests, the persecutions and the opposition they met. They were successful.

> "But the seed on good soil stands for those with a
> noble and good heart, who hear the Word, retain
> it, and *BY PERSEVERING* produce a crop
> (Luke 8:15 NIV).

IN QUICK REVIEW:

1.   If there are no trials, the project probably isn't
     worthwhile.

2.   Jesus never quit.

3.   The double-minded man can expect NOTHING
     of the Lord.

4.   Finish what God guides you to begin.

CHAPTER SIX

YOUR SUCCESS PRINCIPLE FOR TODAY:

Stop Grumbling!

TEXT: *"Stop grumbling among yourselves"* (John 6:43 NIV).

Jesus was teaching the people that He was the Bread of Life which came down from heaven. When He said this, some of the Jews began to complain against Him, not understanding how this could be. As far as they were concerned Jesus was merely the eldest son of Mary and Joseph. They had no revelation as to who He really was.

Like the Pharisees, scores of otherwise intelligent people still grumble and complain about things they do not understand. This is unfortunate. Most folks do not realize that this sort of behavior automatically spells F-A-I-L-U-R-E.

One of the chief causes of defeat among the children of Israel was their sin of grumbling.

"And do not grumble, as some of them did — and were killed by the destroying angel" (1

83

Corinthians 10:10 NIV).

Jude prophesied concerning the doom of "grumblers and faultfinders." (See Jude 16.)

Despite the solemn Bible warnings of failure to the persistent grumbler, thousands of people (even Christians) continue in their ill-habit of squawking and bellyaching about anything they don't understand. They have unconsciously chosen to pursue the road to ruin.

"I can't stand my boss! He isn't fair!"

"Our president is doing a lousy job. If *I* were him . . ."

"There sure are plenty of hypocrites in that church."

"I think that preacher is in the ministry just for the money!"

"Did you hear about so-and-so? Well, I never would have done what she did! She's a real disgrace. . . ."

"I can't understand why Bill got the promotion. He's probably shining the boss's shoes on the side!"

"Our government is run by a bunch of clowns."

Let's face it. People who habitually complain and murmur and grumble are only exposing their own insecurity. Quite often they feel that if they put others down, they will automatically be elevated. The reverse, however, is true. When some person grumbles about another person, it automatically places the grumbler in a bad light.

EMPLOYMENT

One of the danger signals an employer is quick to spot in a job applicant is murmuring. If an applicant grumbles and complains about his previous employer and gripes about his former job, the chances are, he won't get hired. The employer knows that this type of person seldom makes a first class workman.

Realistically speaking, grumblers nearly always fall into the category of the unsuccessful.

AN ILLUSTRATION

At the city glass factory, Barry B. received a promotion with a substantial pay increase. Other employees became jealous and began to grumble against this young man. Some called him "pen-wiper." Others called him "the boss's pet." Still others referred to him with names that no decent, honorable human being would use.

In the midst of their griping, Barry was still the prevailing one. It's no wonder he was chosen for promotion. He was a positive, enthusiastic, cooperative individual, who always strived for ex-

cellence on the job. Never was he heard speaking
badly about anyone . . . including the boss. The
promotion should have gone to him — and it did!
He was the best man for the job.

The others had no right to complain. They too
had a fair chance of getting the promotion. All that
was needed was revised attitudes. You see, these
men were negative, pessimistic, uncooperative
GRUMBLERS! Nobody forced them to be that
way; it was their choice. That's why they didn't get
the job advancement and Barry did.

DON'T BLAME LUCK

When we see successful individuals, there is a
subtle temptation to credit their success to luck.
We think perhaps they had the "lucky breaks" or
knew the right people. But when we verbalize these
thoughts, isn't it actually a form of soft-colored
grumbling? God shows no favoritism (Romans
2:11). What He has done for others, He will do for
you and for me if we will simply follow the instructions.

> "Do everything without complaining or argu-
> ing . . ." (Philippians 2:14 NIV).

Take a good look at the successful leaders you
know of today. You'll notice a quality in their lives
that perhaps you've previously overlooked: they
aren't complainers. You don't hear the *productive*
leader grumbling about the weather, or the secre-

tary, or the staff, or anything else for that matter. If something is not right and can be changed, he accepts the challenge and searches for creative ways of modifying the situation. If it can't be changed, he gracefully accepts it. What good does it do him to grumble and complain?

HOW THE LYRICS OF A SONG HELPED ME

I took my car in to the garage to have a new battery installed recently, and was informed that the job would not be completed for two hours due to the mechanic's heavy work load. At first I was tempted to grumble (because I had such a tight schedule to keep), but remembered a song by Tammy Bakker I had played on our daily radio broadcast. It was called "When Life Hands You a Lemon, Start Makin' Lemonade."* So I decided not to complain, but instead determined to look for an opportunity to turn this "lemon" into "lemonade."

As a flash of inspiration, it occurred to me that there was a Christian bookstore only a few blocks away. So I walked down there, purchased a couple books, and spent the remaining time in the coffee shop catching up on some of my reading.

*From the album *Love Never Gives Up*, by Tammy Bakker, produced by Gary S. Paxton.

As it turned out, I was able to finish reading an entire book before my car was ready. Man, that sure felt good! The time of waiting wasn't wasted by sitting in a chair, thumbing through outdated magazines. Best of all, I felt victorious because I didn't grumble, but with God's help, turned a problem into an opportunity.

Complaining always breeds more complaining. Griping brings discouragement. Murmuring causes division and disunity. How can these things possibly help to make anyone successful? They can't!

"Gentle words cause life and health; griping brings discouragement" (Proverbs 15:4 TLB).

Griping and grumbling, the Bible says, brings DIS-couragement. The successful person is a person of courage. How can an individual maintain the victory if he allows himself to be DIS-couraged by his own mouth?

Sure, there is always something we *could* complain about if we really wanted to. But we'd be operating on a self-actuated failure system if we did.

Jesus could have complained. He could have grumbled about the nails in His feet and hands. I don't suppose they were any too comfortable. Nevertheless, He did not utter one single word of complaint as He hung there dying on the cross.

St. Paul was in jail at Philippi. His back was bleeding. His feet were in stocks and his wrists were chained. It would have been mighty easy in a predicament like that to murmur against God, or complain against the guards, or make a fuss about the situation. But what did this great apostle do? He PRAYED and SANG PRAISES unto God along with his companion, Silas (Acts 16:25). Paul maintained the victory!

You can always recognize the people who are headed for success. They don't grumble. They aren't quick to air their grievances and don't continually register complaints. They are success-bound.

HOW TO AVOID GRUMBLING

1. Look for opportunities in every problem before opening your mouth.

2. Learn the secret of praying and praising God in ALL situations.

Remember, grumbling is a sin that leads to failure.

IN QUICK REVIEW:

1. Grumbling automatically spells F-A-I-L-U-R-E.

2. Complaining exposes a person's insecurity.

3. Successful leaders aren't complainers.

4. Griping brings discouragement.

5. Look for opportunities in every problem.

6. Accept challenges with a positive, enthusiastic attitude.

7. Learn to praise God in EVERY situation.

CHAPTER SEVEN

YOUR SUCCESS PRINCIPLE FOR TODAY:

Let Nothing Be Wasted!

TEXT: *". . . Let nothing be wasted"* (John 6:12).

A miracle had just taken place; a miracle of supply. Only moments prior to Jesus saying, "Let nothing be wasted," He had taken five loaves of bread and two small fish and miraculously fed five thousand hungry men. There were even twelve baskets of food left over after everyone was full!

Jesus always seemed to be able to supply people's needs, no matter what they happened to be. When the taxes were due, Jesus told Peter to go down to the lake and cast in the line. "Take the first fish you catch, open it's mouth and you'll find enough money to pay the taxes." Jesus knew how to get people's needs met.

It mattered not whether someone had a need for healing, forgiveness, clothes, food, or money, Jesus always somehow made the provision. It reminds us of God's Promise of supply in Philippians:

> "But my God shall supply all your need according to His riches in glory BY CHRIST JESUS" (Philippians 4:19).

In any event, Jesus was able to provide for the need even abundantly above all that anyone could ever imagine. This was demonstrated clearly by the "left over" supply of food after the feeding of the multitude.

Notwithstanding the fact that Jesus was (and is) capable of supplying ANYTHING we could ask or think, He nevertheless made a simple, yet profound statement when He said,

> "Let *NOTHING* be wasted!"

This is a tremendous principle of success: WASTE NOTHING! Jesus was teaching us the importance of conserving, saving, and budgeting — yes, even leftovers!

In America we have a tendency to unnecessarily squander many of the precious things God has blessed us with. For example, some people misuse the time God has given them. Others misspend their money. Still others waste food, clothing, and other material goods. Then there are those who are guilty of expending and exhausting their God-given energies on inconsequential, unprofitable activities.

But Jesus said, "LET NOTHING BE WASTED!"

TIME

Let not your time be wasted. The person who plans his day in advance can go about his work in a logical, efficient manner, accomplishing everything he needs to. When there is no daily plan, his schedule will be controlled by problems, circumstances and other people. How a person spends his God-given time now will undoubtedly be a determining factor as to how successful he will be ten years from now, should the Lord tarry.

HOW TO ADD HOURS TO YOUR DAY

"Live life then, with a due sense of responsibility, not as men who do not know the meaning and purpose of life, but as those who do. MAKE THE BEST USE OF YOUR TIME, despite all the difficulties of these days" (Ephesians 5:15-16 Phillips).

"Teach us to number our days and recognize how few they are; HELP US TO SPEND THEM AS WE SHOULD" (Psalm 90:12 TLB).

KEY NUMBER 1 — **Put God first!** (Matthew 6:33)

"Reverence for God ADDS HOURS to each day" (Proverbs 10:27 TLB).

Strange as it may seem, if we will put God FIRST, He will add hours to our day. Of course this doesn't mean you will get 25 or 26 hours a day while others are still getting only 24. It does, however, indicate that you will accomplish more in a 24-hour period if you put God first, than you could if you didn't reverence the Lord.

I used to have a difficult time getting everything done that needed to get done until I learned this fundamental kingdom principle. I would struggle to find time to make our radio broadcasts, write articles for the monthly newsletter, study for teaching lessons, and all the other things that go along with the ministry. I seemingly could make no headway. Then one day, I made the decision to spend an extra hour or so in Bible reading, prayer and meditation every morning — the first thing.

It took discipline. Some mornings I would much rather have stayed in bed, but the commitment was made and with the Lord's help, I was able to stick to it. Soon a miracle began to happen. God started teaching me time management principles that I had never heard of before. I saw things in God's Word I had missed before this. I learned how to schedule my day and set goals and priorities. And today, I have all the time I need to achieve what God has given me to do.

If we don't put God FIRST, we'll find ourselves expending time on insignificant jobs that are unnecessary, unprofitable, and do nothing more than consume our time.

TO ADD HOURS TO YOUR DAY, PUT GOD FIRST.

Key Number 2 — Don't waste time on nonsense!

> ". . . Their prophets worshipped Baal and WASTED THEIR TIME ON NONSENSE" (Jeremiah 2:8 TLB).

> ". . . And walked after things THAT DID NOT PROFIT!" (Jeremiah 2:8 NASB)

My wife and I seldom spend time watching television. We do enjoy watching the Christian programs when we can, but that's about the extent of it. Recently, however, we did allow ourselves to view an evening television drama. We felt that we "deserved a break" that day, so we turned the TV on, sat back, and planned to spend a delightful hour video-gazing.

Well, we learned that the program we had chosen to take in was of no profit whatsoever. It was of no benefit to us spiritually, mentally, physically, financially, or any other way (except to use as a good illustration on how to waste your time). The story was about a homosexual cop and, of course, he was the star of the show; the hero of the story.

Mary Jo (my wife) and I repented that we had allowed an entire hour of God's time to go down the drain.

If a person insists upon squandering his time on things that do not profit, he has no right to complain that he doesn't have enough time to do the things he should.

Before engaging in any time-consuming function, ask yourself these questions:

1. Is this a "nonsense activity?"

2. How will this activity profit the Kingdom of God?

3. How will it profit others?

4. How will it profit me?

5. How does it fit in with God's plan for my life?

To add hours to your day, strip away the "nonsense things" that do not profit.

Key Number 3 — Have a plan for each day.

"A wise man thinks ahead; a fool doesn't and even brags about it" (Proverbs 13:16 TLB).

"We should make our plans counting on God to direct us" (Proverbs 16:9 TLB).

"The plans of the diligent lead to profit" (Proverbs 21:5 NIV).

God works by plans. He had a *plan* for the universe. He had a *plan* for the salvation of the lost.

He has a *plan* for your life and mine. God is organized! Shouldn't we imitate our Heavenly Father and learn the importance of having a plan?

Failing to plan is one of the greatest causes of failure. The person that desires to be useful must develop the ability to make and implement plans. When twenty-five leaders of Christian organizations were asked to list their greatest time thieves, "lack of planning and poor organization" were among the top items entered.

The effective preacher understands the vital importance of proper planning. In fact, preparation is a part of the believers armor listed in Ephesians, chapter six.

". . . And your feet shod with the PREPARA-TION of the gospel of peace" (Ephesians 6:15).

A sermon with no plan or preparation is like a ship without a rudder. It has no direction. Usually it goes around in circles, bores the listener, and fails to accomplish its intended purpose. Any message is severely crippled when there is no plan.

The same is true when there is no plan for our day. We lose direction and end up going around in circles. We find ourselves making the deadly mistake of hitting the problems primarily, rather than the opportunities. Then at the end of the day we feel frustrated, like we haven't achieved anything worthwhile.

HOW TO PLAN YOUR DAY

In planning your day, make a general list of the things you want to get done. For example:

☐ Read Exodus chapter 5.
☐ Read Psalms 1-2
☐ Prayer and Meditation
☐ Take kids to Gramma's
☐ Meeting with Dr. Jacobs (3 p.m.)
☐ Get car washed

After you have made the list, go on to Key Number 4. . . .

Key Number 4 — Set priorities!

"Prepare thy work without, and make it fit for thyself in the field; and AFTERWARDS build thine house" (Proverbs 24:27). (In other words, DO FIRST THINGS FIRST!)

Even nature abides by the law of priorities —

"For the earth bringeth forth fruit of herself; *FIRST* the blade, *THEN* the ear, *AFTER THAT* the full corn in the ear" — Jesus (Mark 4:28).

What is the law of priorities? Simply this: "DO FIRST THINGS FIRST." Do things in the order of their importance.

After you have made a list of the things you'd like to get done on a particular day, number them in the logical order of their importance. Then start doing number one until it's finished (or until you've gone as far as you can for that day). Afterward cross it off your list and proceed to item number two, and so forth. At times you will be tempted to do menial tasks that weren't on your list but you must try to ignore them and keep active on your priority items until they are complete. You might be surprised at what you and Jesus can accomplish in one day's time!

To add hours to your day, set priorities!

Key Number 5 — Try getting by on a little less sleep.

"Do not love sleep or you will grow poor; stay awake and you will have food to spare" (Proverbs 20:13 NIV).

It has been scientifically and medically proven that most of us can get by adequately with less sleep. Jesus sometimes spent entire nights in prayer with apparently no sleep at all (Luke 6:17). Could it be that He found a relaxation and a "strengthening power" in prayer that many individuals today do not understand? Jesus got by on less sleep.

Try getting a half hour less sleep for a couple of weeks. Make sure you give yourself plenty of time to get used to your new schedule before giving up. Use the extra time constructively. Perhaps you could use the extra time to add a dimension to your prayer life. You might want to pray for special missionary projects, or others who you normally don't remember in prayer. Whatever you decide to do with your extra half hour or so, make sure it's positive and constructive. This is important.

The amount of sleep a person needs each night varies from person to person. You may need only five hours, whereas someone else may require seven. You'll have to find out what your individual requirements are.

To add hours to your day, try a little less sleep.

Key Number 6 — Learn to delegate.

Jesus delegated authority to His disciples (Luke 9:1). The apostles had to have delegates to care for the business which they had not the time to handle (Acts 6:1-4). The great leaders of history learned the secret of delegation. A good leader always finds a way to involve others to the extent of their ability.

In the home situation, every family member should have a delegated responsibility. When people have responsibilities, they are happier, more contented individuals. Everybody likes the feeling of belonging. Each person needs to know he has a purpose to fulfill. Delegating chores and tasks to each family member will create an atmosphere of "you belong" — "you're needed."

Face the facts — you can't do everything by yourself. That's why you need a team. Don't be selfish. Let others help you succeed! Others want to help you. At the same time you are helping them. Only a person full of pride tries to hold the reigns of every department. That's a sure road to failure.

Our ministry grew tremendously when I began developing different departments and turning them over to capable, responsible individuals. Let me share what happened in one year's time after I learned the secret of delegation. Our radio broadcast went from a weekly broadcast to a daily broadcast. We were able to produce 25 times more literature (which, incidentally is being distributed throughout the United States and overseas). Our mailing list size quadrupled. We were able to expand our prison ministry. I was able to double my teaching schedule. These are just a few of the benefits we received from delegating.

To add hours to your day, learn to delegate.

Key Number 7 — Learn to say "NO" without feeling guilty.

St. Paul had spent a great deal of time in Ephesus, teaching and enjoying the fellowship of the brethren there. But . . .

"When they desired him to tarry longer time with them, he consented not" (Acts 18:20).

Paul had to say "no" to their invitation. He had goals in other areas to pursue, and felt that God's will was calling him to move on.

I'm sure we all have at one time or another, accepted invitations, not because we "felt the call," but because we would have been embarrassed to say no. This ought not to be.

Mary Jo and I have had to turn down many social invitations simply because our schedule did not permit them. God has given us goals and priorities that we must adhere to if we expect to continue being useful to Him. This is not by any means to say that social events are wrong. Not at all! It's good to get together for fellowship with dear brothers and sisters in the Lord, and certainly we must do this. But what I am talking about are those "on-the-spot" invitations to ice cream parties and similar events. Because of our tight schedule, there is very little time for this type of activity.

When we must turn down invitations, most people are kind enough to understand. All of us must learn to say "no" to things that would put a great deal of strain on our schedules, and things that do not fit into our God-given priorities.

If you want to add hours to your day, learn to say "no."

MONEY

"Let nothing be wasted" . . . including your money!

The Bible gives us a simple plan for making our money stretch. It's called "tithing." That's the process whereby you give 10% of your gross income to your church, and God sees to it that you actually prosper more on the 90% left than you would had you kept the entire 100%.

How does God do it? I don't know, but I know He does!

> "Will a man rob God? Yet ye have robbed Me. But ye say, Wherein have we robbed thee? In tithes and offerings. Ye are cursed with a curse: for ye have robbed me . . . bring ye all the tithes into the storehouse . . . and prove me now herewith saith the Lord of hosts, if I will not open you the windows of heaven and pour you out a blessing, that there shall not be room enough to receive it, and I will rebuke the devourer for your sakes, and he shall not destroy the fruits of your ground . . . saith the Lord of hosts" (Malachi 3:8-11).

People who have been dedicated tithers, never have any desire to cease the practice. They have learned that when they tithe:

1. God blesses them beyond all human comprehension (Malachi 3:10).

2. God (if they persist in tithing) causes things to last longer and prevents pests from destroying their property (Malachi 3:11).

3. God will eventually give them greater prosperity (Proverbs 3:9-10).

4. The tither has a storehouse of treasure in heaven (Luke 12:32-34).

5. The tither finds it easier to submit to God in other areas of his (or her) life. The tither has learned to put God first!

"The purpose of tithing is to teach you always to put God FIRST in your lives" (Deuteronomy 14:23 TLB).

If a person REALLY believes the Bible, he will give to God at least ten percent of his gross income. He doesn't want to miss the blessings that are promised to the faithful tither.

Do you want to quit wasting money? Then start by tithing. God can teach you how to make your pennies stretch. Look at the life of Abraham. He was a tither. This is what God did in his life:

". . . The Lord had blessed him in every way" (Genesis 24:1 NIV).

"The Lord blessed my master (Abraham) abundantly, and he has become wealthy. He has given him sheep and cattle, silver and gold, menservants and maidservants, and camels and donkeys" (Genesis 24:35 NIV).

Isaac also was undoubtedly a tither.

"Isaac planted crops in that land and THE SAME YEAR reaped a hundredfold, because the Lord had blessed him. The man became rich, and his wealth continued to grow until he became very wealthy" (Genesis 26:12-13 NIV).

God promised to rebuke the devourer for our sakes if we will give to His work first. If we try to pay the bills, buy the groceries, pay the taxes, and make the repairs first, we'll discover that for some strange reason, more things begin to break down, the groceries cost more, and we seem to have more and more problems.

Today many people try to work things backwards from the way the Bible teaches. They say, "Well, when God makes me rich, then I'll give to Him." My friend, that's not God's plan!

God said to give to Him FIRST, then He will bless you with so many blessings, you'll hardly be able to stand them all! Once again, the law of priorities is in effect.

Not many years ago in Seoul, Korea, the esteemed Dr. Paul Yonggi Cho taught the principles of Biblical tithing to his congregation. Six poor peasant men applied these principles, put them into practice, and today are millionaires. Stop wasting your money — start tithing.

I remember a time before I got married when I didn't think I had enough money to buy groceries.

I thought about "borrowing" my tithe money, but knew that God wanted the FIRST of my income, not the leftovers. So I went ahead and gave to God. When I went to the store, you should have seen the deals I got. I remember a bottle of deodorant I bought: It was in the same rack with all the other regular kinds of deodorant, only this one particular bottle was marked half price. I grabbed it and said, "Thank you, Lord," and continued to get bargains like you wouldn't believe! It was terrific.

By giving to God FIRST, you can get by on $10.00 better than you can on $20.00 when you don't give to God first. Just ask any dedicated tither. They'll tell you.

On another occasion, Mary Jo and I were trying to catch up on the bills from our wedding. We figured we owed about $800.00 . . . and we didn't have it. (Does this sound familiar?) So we scraped together $8.00, gave it to a work of God, and within two weeks the full $800.00 came in and our bills were miraculously paid off in full.

Jesus said, "Let nothing be wasted."

Don't waste your money. Become a faithful tither — and watch the windows of heaven open up for you.

Your success principle from the lips of Jesus for today is: LET NOTHING BE WASTED!

Don't waste your money — be a tither!

Don't waste your time — budget it!

Don't waste your talent — use it!

Don't waste your faith — exercise it!

Don't waste your life — give it to Jesus!

Don't waste this book — share it with a friend!

IN QUICK REVIEW:

1. How a person spends his time now will undoubtedly be a determining factor as to how successful he will be ten years from now.

2. How to add hours to your day:
   (a) Put God FIRST.
   (b) Don't waste time on nonsense.
   (c) Plan your day.
   (d) Set priorities.
   (e) Get a little less sleep, if possible.
   (f) Delegate.
   (g) Learn to say "no."

3. For financial prosperity, become a tither!
   (a) Give God at least 10% of your gross income.

CHAPTER EIGHT

YOUR SUCCESS PRINCIPLE
FOR TODAY:

Do Things God's Way!

TEXT: *"I tell you the truth, the man who does not enter the sheep pen by the gate, but climbs in some other way, is a thief and a robber"* (John 10:1 NIV).

Jesus told us that He is the Gate to the sheep pen; the only entrance into the fold. We are cautioned not to even attempt to enter in any other way lest we be classified as thieves and robbers. And we know that thieves and robbers are on the road to eternal failure.

Believe it or not, there are people today who are trying to gain entrance into heaven SOME OTHER WAY than God's way. To them, anything would be more acceptable than admitting their sin, guilt, and need of repentance. Some people are embarrassed to say the Name "Jesus" let alone accept Him as their Lord and Saviour. But the Bible offers only one way to heaven:

"Jesus saith unto him, I am the way, the truth, and the life: no man cometh unto the Father, but by me" (John 14:6).

"If thou shalt CONFESS WITH THY MOUTH the Lord Jesus, and shalt BELIEVE IN THINE HEART that God hath raised Him from the dead, thou shalt be saved" (Romans 10:9).

The born-again believer knows there is only one way to receive eternal life — God's way! That is, by repenting of sins and fully trusting in Christ's shed blood. There just isn't any other way. If a person tries to gain entrance into heaven apart from Jesus Christ, his efforts will certainly fail.

SUCCESS — GOD'S WAY!

As unpleasant as it is, there are many (even Spirit-filled believers) who haven't learned the success principle of doing *EVERYTHING* God's way. Thousands of individuals, though they have entered the "sheep pen" through the Gate (Jesus Christ), are still scrambling for temporal success their OWN WAY instead of GOD'S WAY. But it can't be done!

1. **Some think they can be successful in life without praying.** But God says:

   "Ye have not because ye ask not" (James 4:2).

   "*A*SK and it shall be given you; *S*EEK and ye shall find; *K*NOCK and it shall be opened unto you" (Matthew 7:7).

"Don't worry about anything; instead pray about everything" (Philippians 4:6 TLB).

2. **Some believe they can live a life of victory while still allowing pride to remain in their lives.** But that is not God's way.

"Pride goeth before destruction. . . . (Proverbs 16:18).

"A man's pride shall bring him low. . . . (Proverbs 29:23).

"Wisdom hates pride, arrogance, corruption and deceit of any kind" (Proverb 8:13 TLB).

"You have been fooled by your fame and your pride" (Jeremiah 49:16 TLB).

The Pharisees were real losers. They were full of pride (Luke 11:43, Mark 12:38-40).

The Antichrist will come in great pride (2 Thessalonians 2:4, Daniel, chapter 8). Though experiencing what appears to be a great success, he will eventually lose everything — for eternity!

Do you want the Lord to lift you up? If so, follow His instructions:

"Humble yourselves in the sight of the Lord, and He shall lift you up" (James 4:10).

"Humble yourselves, therefore, under the mighty hand of God, that He may exalt you in due time" (1 Peter 5:6).

3. **Some think that just because they are Christians, success should automatically flow to**

them. They don't move ahead because they don't meet the conditions. In the Bible, God's people were always required to use their faith + action in order to obtain the promises. Faith is believing what God's Word says AND DOING IT! Here's God's way:

"This Book of the Law (the Bible) shall not depart out of thy mouth; but thou shalt meditate therein day and night, that thou mayest observe to do according to all that is written therein: for *THEN* thou shalt make thy way prosperous, and *THEN* thou shalt have good success" (Joshua 1:8).

Notice these three key points:

You must:

1. SPEAK THE WORD
2. MEDITATE ON THE WORD
3. DO THE WORD

I call your attention also to the fact that *YOU* shall make your way prosperous if these conditions are met. Don't wait for God to come down and clunk you on the head with success. He doesn't do it that way. *You* have to make your way successful by speaking, meditating upon, and doing the Word of God.

"But be ye DOERS of the Word and not hearers only, deceiving your own selves" (James 1:22).

The person who HEARS the Word, but never DOES the Word, is SELF-DECEIVED. Success can't come to a person like that. The Word of God must be acted upon in order to be effective in a person's life.

4. **Other folks try to gain success while still allowing selfishness to dominate their lives.** Their "way" never works. The selfish person and the victorious Christian are never the same person.

It's easy to locate the selfish person. He is always talking about *HIM*-self. You'll hear him boasting about *HIS* projects, *HIS* plans, *HIS* troubles, *HIS* achievements, *HIS* aches and pains, *HIS* opinions, *HIS* position, and *HIS* awards. He doesn't listen to the other fellow because he's so much more important! You can spot him in a flash. But selfishness is not God's way to success. God's way is:

> "Don't think only of yourself. Try to think of the other fellow too, and what is best for him" (1 Corinthians 10:24 TLB).

> "If any man will come after Me, let him DENY HIMSELF, and take up his cross, and follow Me" — Jesus (Matthew 16:24).

5. **Some try to succeed while employing undue confidence in SELF, instead of placing full confidence in GOD.** But God's way is:

"Rejoice in Christ Jesus and HAVE NO CON-
FIDENCE IN THE FLESH" (Philippians 3:3).

". . . Your faith should *NOT* stand in the
wisdom of men, but in the power of God" (1
Corinthians 2:5).

"The Lord will be your confidence and will
keep your foot from being snared" (Psalm 3:26
NIV).

6.   **Some people try to live a prevailing life
      while continuing to be lazy.** But that is not
      God's way!

See Proverbs 24:30-34. God guarantees poverty
and scarcity to the lazy person.

"One who is slack in his work is brother to one
who destroys" (Proverbs 18:9 NIV).

7.   **Some well-meaning Christians make the
      mistake of accepting materialism as a sign
      of true success.** This is not God's way.

Esau sold his birthright for a morsel of food.
He is a type of those people who place a higher
value on temporal, material belongings than they
do eternal things.

Being earthly-minded, Esau did not com-
prehend the spiritual value of his birthright. As the
first-born, he inherited the right to receive the
promises given to his grandfather, Abraham, but
because of his lack of faith and concern only about
the "here and now," he could not see the pre-
ciousness of his birthright until after it was too

late.

> "Lest there be any fornicator of profane person, as Esau, who for one morsel of meat sold his birthright. For ye know that how afterward, when he would have inherited the blessing, he was rejected: for he found no place of repentance, though he sought it carefully with tears" (Hebrews 12:16-17).

This is not to say that God doesn't delight in the material prosperity of His children, because He does.

> ". . . No good thing will He withhold from them that walk uprightly" (Psalm 84:11).

> ". . . Let the Lord be magnified, which hath pleasure in the prosperity of His servant" (Psalm 35:27).

> "Beloved, I wish above all things that thou mayest prosper and be in health, even as thy soul prospereth" (3 John 2).

God is delighted when we have "things," but wants us to maintain the proper priorities. We must seek FIRST His kingdom, and not the kingdom of "things." Things will come, but God's kingdom, and His righteousness must be placed first in our lives.

> "But seek ye first the kingdom of God, and His righteousness; and all these *things* shall be added unto you" (Matthew 6:33).

> "The Lord is my Shepherd, I shall *lack nothing*" (Psalm 23:1 NIV).

8. **Some people think the way to success is to give as little as possible and to get all they can while the "gettin' is good!"** But that is not God's way either.

   "*Give* and it shall be given you" (Luke 6:38).

   "Honor the Lord with your wealth, with the firstfruits of all your crops; *THEN* your barns will be filled to overflowing, and your vats will brim over with new wine" (Proverbs 3:9-10 NIV).

   "A generous man will himself be blessed for he shares his food with the poor" (Proverbs 22:9 NIV).

   "A stingy man is eager to get rich and is unaware that poverty awaits him" (Proverbs 28:22 NIV).

9. **Multiplied thousands of people fail because they continue in sin, making excuses for it instead of renouncing it.** Or worse yet, some actually try to cover up their sin. But that is not God's way to success!

   ". . . He that covereth his sins shall not prosper" (Proverbs 28:13).

   But . . .

   "If we confess our sins, He is faithful and just to forgive us our sins, and to cleanse us from all unrighteousness" (1 John 1:9).

10. **Some think that success will come to them if they just do everything they "have to."** But

that's not God's way. God wants us to go the "extra mile" (Matthew 5:41). *Anybody* can do just what is required. That is no great thing. The victory-minded person is the one who does more than what is expected of him. For example, if the "punch out time" is four o'clock, and the work isn't quite finished, he'll stay a few extra minutes to complete the task if necessary. Yes, even on his own time.

The key is to do more than what is expected of you. Always strive for excellence and do the unexpected. That is, do little extras that are not expected. For example, on the way home from work, stop and buy your wife a little gift when she doesn't expect it. Or, if necessary, work a half hour overtime and don't charge the boss. This is "going the extra mile."

Sure, this may mean we'll have to give up some of our time for somebody else. It may mean a little extra labor for us, but it will pay rich rewards. One common denominator of the most successful men of history was their willingness to do more than what was expected of them.

God did this. He applied His own principle. The Messiah was expected to come, but who would have thought that He would be God, Himself, in human form? God did more than we expected of him.

DAVID'S MEN

> "They were armed with bows and could see BOTH the right hand and the left in hurling stones and shooting arrows . . . one of the least was over an hundred, and the greatest over a thousand" (1 Chronicles 12:2, 14).

David's men applied this principle of going the extra mile. The least among them was greater than a hundred ordinary warriors, and the greatest among them was superior to a thousand common, everyday soldiers. Why? Because they did a little extra — they learned to use their left hands as well as their right, something the average fighting man didn't do. No, David's men were not satisfied with mediocrity. They had to be the BEST!

Another fellow that applied this principle was Hanani. Why do you suppose he was chosen to be in charge of Jerusalem during the rebuilding of the wall? Because he went the "extra mile." He was a man of integrity and feared God MORE THAN MOST MEN DO (Nehemiah 7:2). He put a little "extra" into his fellowship with God.

It isn't difficult to recognize the person who is on the way to becoming successful in life. He enthusiastically goes the "extra mile" in every task he sets his hands to.

The person who will only do what he is paid for is headed for a lifetime of failure. "Sure," he says, "I could do a better job if they paid me for it, but

only a fool does something he's not paid for."
That is the losing attitude. It's not God's way. God
said:

> "Whoever sows sparingly will also reap spar-
> ingly, and whoever sows generously will also
> reap generously" (2 Corinthians 9:6).

If you sow seeds of mediocrity, you will reap a
life of mediocrity. If you sow seeds of excellence,
you will reap a life of excellence. It's God's un-
changing, eternal Law — the Law of sowing and
reaping.

Put an extra spark of enthusiasm into your
marriage and watch things perk up. Try to think of
ways of doing things just a little better. Imagine
different methods of adding that extra touch of
special treatment for your spouse and watch your
marriage come alive with new excitement. It really
works.

Do you own a restaurant? Try serving *real*
mashed potatoes. People will know the difference
and will start gossiping about the place that serves
REAL mashed potatoes! Look for little "extras"
you can give the customer. Go the "extra mile."

11. **Some people compromise with the ungodly
and wonder why their lives are failing.** Others
continually mock, scorn, and slander people,
and then wonder why they seemingly cannot
maintain the victory. You see, they are not
doing things God's way. They are operating

some other way.

See 1 Chronicles 5:24-26. This tells of some talented men who had great reputations. But the enemy destroyed them because they failed to do things GOD'S way! They compromised with the ungodly!

See Psalm 1:1-3. Here, one of the main success principles is to not "sitteth in the seat of the scornful." Some translations say essentially not to be a mocker if you want to prosper. People who have scornful, mocking, slanderous attitudes very seldom experience success.

Do things GOD'S WAY if you want to be successful!

"For my thoughts are not your thoughts, neither are your ways, my way, saith the Lord" (Isaiah 55:8).

We all want to bring glory to God by being successful and victorious in this life. But we must learn to do things God's way. Sometimes it takes longer, but the pay-off is eternal. Anyone who tries another way is a thief and a robber on the path to defeat.

Your success principle for today: DO THINGS GOD'S WAY!

IN QUICK REVIEW:

1. Jesus is the only Way to the Father.

2. Prayer is vital to success.

3. Stay humble.

4. Speak the Word, meditate upon the Word, and *DO* the Word.

5. Place no confidence in the flesh.

6. Laziness brings poverty.

7. Don't mistake materialism for true success.

8. Give and it shall be given you.

9. Go the extra mile in everything you do. Strive for excellence.

10. Do things God's way!

CHAPTER NINE

YOUR SUCCESS PRINCIPLE FOR TODAY:

Be A Pacesetter!

TEXT: ". . . *He goes on ahead of them, and His sheep follow Him . . .*" (John 10:4 NIV).

Jesus was speaking of the Good Shepherd, how He goes ahead of the sheep and they follow.

Jesus was a leader; a pacesetter! Not swayed by the opinions of men (Mark 12:14), He continuously moved in a positive direction toward fulfilling His purpose. He didn't let other people do His thinking for Him. Even in the midst of controversy and criticism, Jesus kept moving. He kept leading.

A Christian is a follower of Jesus Christ, but more than that, should be a leader of men. God desires the Christian to be a leader (Hebrews 5:12). He doesn't want us to simply follow the crowd, or follow the "traditions of the elders." (See Mark, chapter 7.) He has called us to step out, step up, and be the leaders he intended us to be.

Real pacesetters follow Jesus Christ, but go on ahead of others and take the lead by listening to God's voice; not getting trapped by tradition, or the "we've-never-done-it-that-way-before" attitude. Pacesetters aren't afraid of moving into new faith ventures never before tried.

A good example of real pacesetters is found in the field of television evangelism. When Christians first began to employ this method of sharing the Gospel, scores of spiritual leaders cried out against it. "Worldliness, worldliness," they rang out. But the real pacesetters didn't let that stop them. They had heard from God, and planned to persevere in this new venture until success was realized. They stuck to it, boring up under the pressure of criticism. Who will argue with the fact that today television is a highly effective tool of evangelism? Every day hundreds are coming to know the Lord Jesus Christ in a personal way because they heard the Gospel on television and their faith was triggered to accept God's grace.

DIFFERENCE BETWEEN GENUINE AND MAKE-BELIEVE LEADERS

There is a distinct difference between a genuine pacesetter and a make-believe leader. Let's take a look at a few of them:

An Authentic Leader:	A Synthetic Leader:
1. follows Jesus Christ.	1. follows selfish ambition.
2. leads	2. coerces, forces, pushes.
3. takes time to listen to others because people are important.	3. just waits his turn to talk because he feels he is so important.
4. sees problems as exciting challenges.	4. sees every problem as an immovable mountain.
5. desires to be successful because of his love for God and mankind.	5. pushes for success out of selfish ambition.
6. moves in faith when he is sure God is guiding.	6. says, "But we've never done it that way before!"
7. desires to please God more than anyone else.	7. tries to please himself first. God and others are always last.
8. listens to the advice of godly people.	8. knows it all already. Just ask him!
9. says, "All things are possible to him that believes!"	9. says, "That's impossible!"
10. is willing to pay the price of being a genuine pacesetter.	10. is always looking for a short-cut to success.

Jesus, in His earthly ministry, was a genuine, authentic pacesetter. To Him, it made no difference what the customs were, if somebody needed something He could supply, He'd do it! For example, if somebody needed healing, Jesus healed them. Of course it brought much criticism to His ministry because He healed people on the Sabbath Day, which was against their tradition. But the persecution didn't upset Jesus — He was a Pacesetter!

You can be a genuine pacesetter too! So what if nobody else believes and acts upon God's Word for what it says? — You be a winner, and do it! Don't let other people mold you into their image; let God mold you into His Image (2 Corinthians 3:18).

A CLOSER LOOK

Let's take a closer look at some of the characteristics of an outstanding leader:

1. **The really great leader has the DESIRE to be a good leader.**

Solomon was this type of person. He desired to be an effective leader, so he prayed for special wisdom and knowledge to help him.

> "Give me an understanding mind so that I can govern your people well and know the difference between what is right and what is wrong. For who by himself is able to carry such a heavy responsibility?" (1 Kings 3:9 TLB)

God granted Solomon's request and caused him to become a powerful, successful leader in his day. Remember, it all began with Solomon's *DESIRE* to be an effective leader. If he hadn't desired it, he wouldn't have prayed for wisdom and knowledge on how to handle such a solemn responsibility. He desired to be a good leader, therefore, would not be satisfied with mediocrity, but wanted the best possible help he could get to do the job, which, of course, was God's wisdom and knowledge.

When a person desires something strongly enough, and it conforms to God's purposes, all of heaven's forces will come to his aid in fulfilling that desire.

Real pacesetters — the leaders — have a *DESIRE* to lead.

2. **The really great leader realizes that only God can make him great in the eyes of the people.** No pushing, no striving for the top seat, no pulling for power, but trusting God makes the real leader move ahead.

    "On that day the Lord magnified Joshua in the sight of all Israel; and they feared him, as they had feared Moses, all the days of his life" (Joshua 4:14).

In this verse, we are told that it was *THE LORD* who magnified Joshua in the sight of the people. It was God who confirmed that this man was indeed the new leader of Israel. Joshua never tried to promote himself or glorify himself before the people. God had chosen him. He was just an ordinary man who was committed to God and believed in pushing for excellence. The Lord revealed to the people of Israel that this was to be their new leader following the death of Moses. Joshua didn't force his way into a leadership position.

Let's talk for a minute about "leadership by force." This is the kind of leadership where a man forces his way (either through "muscle power" or deception) into a position of high rank, then controls the people, the company, or the country on his terms. Quite often this type person will operate his regime using tactics of fear in order to pursue his selfish ambitions.

Adolph Hitler was a classic example of leadership by force. He was not a genuine leader, motivated by love; he was a false leader, motivated by selfish ambition. This egotistic aspiration led to his ruin.

Leadership by force cannot endure. Although, as in the case of Adolph Hitler, temporary success may be achieved, history has shown that this type of leadership is not lasting. The person who uses this method will eventually meet destruction. People will not follow forced leadership forever.

The only true kind of leadership, which is lasting, is leadership by consent of the followers. This is the Jesus-kind of leadership. He said it:

> "As you know, the kings and great men of the earth lord it over the people; but among you IT IS DIFFERENT" (Mark 10:42-43 TLB).

The really great leader does not push for the top by stepping on and stepping over anyone who gets in his way. He realizes that God has to do the promoting, therefore, he keeps his life in harmony with God's plan.

> "For promotion cometh neither from the east, nor from the west, nor from the south. But God is the

Judge; He putteth down one, and setteth up another" (Psalms 75:6-7).

Pacesetters — the real leaders — realize that only God can make them great in the eyes of the people.

3.   **A good leader will pray for his followers and teach them the right way to live.**

Samuel was such a leader.

". . . God forbid that I should sin against the Lord in ceasing to pray for you: but I will teach you the good and the right way" (1 Samuel 12:23).

Jesus prayed for His followers.

"Simon, Simon, behold, Satan hath desired to have you, that he may sift you as wheat: But I have prayed for thee, that thy faith faileth not" (Luke 22:31-32).

"Neither pray I for these alone, but for them also which shall believe on me through their word; that they all may be one" (John 17:20-21).

A genuine leader — a pacesetter — will always pray for his followers.

4.   **A good leader shares. He shares the credits, the honors, and the profits with his team members.**

David was such a leader.

". . . We share and share alike" (1 Samuel 30:24 TLB).

5.   **A genuine leader — a pacesetter — will operate by integrity, not merely by the opinions of other people.** Jesus was this type of leader (and still is).

Even the people who didn't like Him had to admit these three things about Him:

1. He was a man of integrity.
2. He wasn't swayed by what men thought.
3. He sincerely taught the ways of God in accordance with the truth.
   (Mark 12:14 NIV)

6.   **A successful leader must be full of courage and boldness.**

"Be strong and brave, for you will be a successful leader of my people" (Joshua 1:6 TLB).

Joshua certainly was a successful leader in his day. Under his leadership, Israel experienced some of the greatest success and prosperity in their history. They were continually conquering new territories and moving ahead with God. Joshua was a real leader; an authentic pacesetter, full of courage and boldness, unafraid to stand up for what he believed in. He displayed an unwavering trust in the Lord in spite of adverse conditions. He was a genuine leader.

Nobody wants to follow a leader that lacks courage. It takes courage to step out on the Promises of God. It takes courage to dream big dreams and make big plans. It takes courage to confess with your mouth what you believe in your heart. Who wants to follow a timid, cowardly individual who is afraid to believe and act upon the Promises of God?

A successful leader must be full of courage!

7. **A legitimate leader will be fair and just in all matters.**

    "Evil men don't understand the importance of justice, but *those who follow the Lord* are much concerned about it" (Proverbs 28:5 TLB).

    "A just king gives stability to his nation" (Proverbs 29:4 TLB).

    "How can you claim that you belong to the Lord Jesus Christ, the Lord of glory, if you show favoritism to rich people and look down on poor people?" (James 2:1 TLB)

8. **A true leader will accept the blame when things go wrong.** This separates the successful leaders from the unsuccessful. The failing "leader" will always blame something or someone else when trouble comes. He will try to blame "luck," the devil, or someone else, but certainly *he* is never to blame (just ask him).

In contrast to the phoney leader, the genuine pacesetter assumes full responsibility for his mistakes. He doesn't look for someone else to blame. The good teacher will not blame the students if half of them are sleeping during class. He (or she) will ask, "What's wrong with my teaching?" "Am I boring?" "What creative teaching methods can I use to keep the students awake?" This is a mark of genuine leadership.

The unsuccessful person — the one who never seems to achieve anything of significance, invariably blames other people for his failures. If only he realized how small this makes him look.

I remember a minister who found the church attendance way down. What did he do? Did he ask "What am I doing wrong?" Did he pray for creative ways of getting through to the people? No! He first blamed the people for putting the church in "second place." He would even come up with some pretty good sermons on "not forsaking the assembling of ourselves." Secondly, he blamed the board of deacons and trustees. "They should be better spiritual leaders! It's up to them to get the people in here and to set a good example." This poor preacher blamed everybody and everything except himself. No wonder the church hasn't grown in years.

The genuine spiritual giants are those who have learned to accept the blame when things don't go right. David, that great Old Testament leader of Israel, was such a leader. When he saw the angel of destruction with his hand stretched out toward Jerusalem, he spoke to the Lord and said, "Lo, *I* have sinned, and *I* have done wickedly. But these sheep, what have they done? Let thine hand, I pray thee, be against *me*. . . ." (2 Samuel 24:17). David was taking the blame for the fact that destruction was coming. He admitted his guilt; he didn't try to cover it up, or blame someone else. He was a spiritual giant — a man after God's own heart (1 Samuel 13:14).

A genuine leader — a pacesetter — will be willing to accept the blame when things go wrong for which he is responsible.

MORE QUALITIES OF GENUINE LEADERSHIP

At a recent meeting of our board of directors, I asked the question, "What do you consider to be some of the greatest qualities of a good leader?" The directors each answered by giving me two or three characteristics which they considered to be of utmost importance. Then I asked others the same question (my wife, the insurance man, my students, etc.). Here is the combined response:

QUALITIES OF A GREAT LEADER

1. He lives close to God.
2. He listens to others, but is not swayed by their opinions.
3. He seeks and follows the Lord's guidance.
4. He is submissive to his leaders.
5. He sees opportunities in every problem.
6. He is joyful and enthusiastic.
7. He is dedicated, committed, and wholehearted.
8. He is a soulwinner.

9. He develops the ability to inspire others to action.

10. He gains a knowledge of his calling, position, or occupation.

11. He displays confidence in others by delegating authority and responsibility to capable individuals.

12. He exhibits the love of God in his life.

13. He is someone his subordinates can rely upon.

14. He sticks to his word and keeps his commitments.

15. He is open, sincere, and honest.

16. He exercises discipline and self-control.

17. He does not compromise his principles.

18. He is willing to pay the price of true leadership.

19. He is decisive.

20. He is victory-minded.

Jesus called you to be a leader! If you are a husband, you are to be the leader in the home. If you are a woman, you can be a leader of women. If you are a businessman, you can be a pacesetter in that business. Don't settle for less than God's best. Be a pacesetter! Step out from the crowd and let your life be a living example of what Christ taught. You *can* do it . . . with Christ living in you.

Your success principle for today: BE A PACE-SETTER!

IN QUICK REVIEW:

1. You *CAN* be a real leader!

2. Don't be caught in the trap of "we've-never-done-it-that-way-before."

3. Develop the *DESIRE* to be an effective leader.

4. Only God can make you great in the eyes of the people.

5. Pray for your followers.

6. Share the credits and honors with your team.

7. Live by integrity and don't be swayed by the opinions of others.

8. Develop courage and boldness.

9. Be fair and just.

10. Accept the blame when things go wrong.

CHAPTER TEN

YOUR SUCCESS PRINCIPLE
FOR TODAY:

Love Never Fails!

TEXT: "*. . . Love each other as I have loved you*"
(John 15:12 NIV).

Love is God's plan that is guaranteed never to
fail. Without this success principle in operation, all
the others will not function properly.

"Love *NEVER* fails" (1 Corinthians 13:8
NIV).

Jesus gave us the supreme success principle
when He said "LOVE . . ." All the Law and the
Prophets hang on this commandment of love. Love
is the fulfillment of the Law. All true faith operates
and is motivated by love.

". . . All we need is faith working through
love" (Galatians 5:6 TLB).

"Jesus said unto him, Thou shalt love the
Lord, thy God, with all thy heart, and with all
thy soul, and with all thy mind. This is the first
and greatest commandment. And the second is

like it, Thou shalt love thy neighbor as thyself. On these two commandments hang all the Law and the Prophets'' (Matthew 22:37-40).

''Love worketh no ill to its neighbor; therefore, love is the fulfilling of the Law'' (Romans 13:10).

What kind of love are we talking about here? What type of love is it that never fails? Is it human love, which is often spelled L-U-S-T? No, it's not that kind. Is it the sort of love that has strings attached and says, ''I'll love you if . . . ?'' No. It's not that kind of love either.

This type of love which is guaranteed never to fail is God's kind of love. It is the kind of love that is shed abroad in the hearts of believers everywhere (Romans 5:5). This love is God's guaranteed plan for success that never fails.

Let's take a closer look at this plan called love.

First of all, let's begin by taking a look at God's description of love. (See 1 Corinthians 13:4-7 TLB).

1. Love is patient.

2. Love is kind.

3. Love is never jealous.

4. Love is never envious.

5. Love is never boastful.

6. Love is never proud.

7. Love is never haughty.

8. Love is never selfish.

9. Love is never rude.

10. Love does not demand its own way.

11. Love is not irritable.

12. Love is not touchy.

13. Love does not hold grudges.

14. Love hardly even notices when others do it wrong.

15. Love is never glad about injustice.

16. Love rejoices when the truth wins out.

17. Love is loyal.

18. Love believes in the beloved.

19. Love expects the best of the beloved.

20. Love always stands its ground in defending the beloved.

There is God's description of the kind of love that never fails.

Check your success quotient. Insert your name in front of each description and see how successful you are. For example, "Dave is patient. Dave is kind. Dave is never jealous . . . etc." This will show us areas we need to pray for God's help in our lives and help us to yield those areas to the

Holy Spirit.

The Bible has even more to say about this kind of love.

1.   IT IS LOVE FOR ENEMIES!

". . . Love your enemies" (Matthew 5:44a).

During the Revolutionary War period, there lived a Baptist preacher named Peter Miller. In his hometown of Ephrata, seventy miles from Philadelphia, lived Mike Whittman, an enemy of the cross who took a satanic delight in opposing, criticizing, and persecuting the Baptist minister.

Whittman became involved in some activities against the country, was arrested for treason, and sentenced to die. When the preacher heard about it, he immediately started walking the seventy miles to Philadelphia, hoping to be granted an audience with George Washington. When the interview was given, Miller pleaded for the life of the traitor.

Washington said in response, "Reverend Miller, I'm sorry. I can't pardon the man just because he's a friend of yours."

"Friend?" exclaimed the preacher. "Why, he's one of my most bitter enemies!"

"What?" cried Washington. "You came on foot seventy miles to plead for the life of an enemy?"

Washington was so touched by Miller's demonstration of love for his enemy that he granted the pardon.

Later, Reverend Miller talked with Whittman, following his release, and was able to lead him to eternal life in Jesus Christ, the Lord. You see, Brother Miller operated his "soul-winning program" on the plan that never fails — LOVE!

PRISONER OF WAR

Following World War II, many of the liberated inmates of German concentration camps died in spite of the food and medical aid they received. They seemed broken and bitter.

One of the prisoners, however, was different. There was a smile on his face, a twinkle in his eyes, and energy in his soul. Medical aids were surprised to learn that the man had been in the camp for six years. Prior to that, his wife and five children had been brutally murdered by Nazi soldiers.

But he didn't hate the Nazis. He had seen how hatred destroyed other people, and instead of hating the Nazis for what they had done, he made the decision to love every person he came in contact with. That meant the guards, the German people, the officers, the fellow inmates — everyone! He was determined not to allow bitterness and hatred to destroy him.

This man lived on while others died. Why? Because he chose to operate on God's plan that is guaranteed never to fail.

"Love your enemies, do good to them which hate you" (Luke 6:27).

2. THIS LOVE IS UNCONDITIONAL

"But God commendeth His love toward us, in that, while we were yet sinners, Christ died for us" (Romans 5:8).

Children can be a source of grief to their parents. Such was the case with a particular Christian lady I know. Her son, rebelling against the "system," grew long hair, listened to wild music, refused to work, and started chumming around with the wrong crowd.

Being a devout Christian, this was all very disturbing to the mother. She would nag, "Why don't you go to church?" Whenever rock and roll music albums were found in the house, she would destroy them. All this caused the young man to become increasingly rebellious. The more she nagged, the worse he became.

One night at church the Holy Spirit gently spoke to the heart of this precious mother and said,

"I want you to go home and tell your son that you love him. You haven't told him that since he was just a little fellow. Remember, My love is unconditional; it doesn't change just because a person's hair style changes."

That night she walked into the house. Sonny was sitting there watching a television program. She walked over, sat on the arm of the chair by her son and said, "Sonny, I want you to know that I love you. I haven't told you that in many years, and I apologize. My love for you, Sonny, is unconditional. No, I don't approve of some of the things you are doing with your life, but that doesn't alter my love for you. I just wanted you to know that."

After breathing these tender words to the young man, she left the room, never to nag him again.

Two weeks later, Sonny asked if he could go to church with his mom. "Of course," she gladly consented. That night the boy gave his heart and life to Jesus Christ, gave up his old way of life, and became a brand new creation (2 Corinthians 5:17)! Today, as I am writing this, Sonny is a powerful minister of the Gospel, working with a well-known outreach ministry.

The mother quit operating on what *she* thought was right, and started operating on God's plan that is guaranteed never to fail.

NUISANCE

Do you know why some people make a nuisance of themselves? Quite often it's because they've never before experienced genuine love and are willing to do anything, including become a nuisance, in order to get attention.

Do you know why God allows these people to come our way? It's so we can practice loving them. It's easy to love lovable people. But God's kind of love — the kind that never fails — loves even the unlovable.

3.   **THIS KIND OF LOVE IS SACRIFICIAL**

"For God *so loved* the world, that *He gave* His only begotten Son, that whosoever believeth in Him should not perish, but have everlasting life" (John 3:16).

What could possibly be a better illustration of a giving love than that of our Precious Lord Jesus?

Yes, LOVE is God's plan for success that is guaranteed never to fail. It's no wonder St. Paul said, "Let love be your greatest aim. . . ." (1 Corinthians 14:1 TLB).

"There are three things that remain — faith, hope, and love — and the greatest of these is love" (1 Corinthians 13:13 TLB).

Your success principle for today: Love as Jesus loves.

IN QUICK REVIEW:

1.   Love *never* fails.

2.   Love is not spelled L-U-S-T.

3.   Love is described in 1 Corinthians 13.

4.   Love your enemies . . . and succeed.

5. If you are a believer, love is already in your heart (Romans 5:5), whether you feel it or not.

6. Only YOU can make the decision to love.

7. True love has no strings attached — it's unconditional.

8. True love gives of itself — it is sacrificial.

Necessary Steps to Salvation

1. *ACKNOWLEDGE:* "For all have sinned and come short of the glory of God" (Romans 3:23). "God be merciful to me a sinner" (Luke 18:13). You must acknowledge in the light of God's Word that you are a sinner.

2. *REPENT:* "Except ye repent, ye shall all likewise perish" (Luke 13:3). "Repent ye therefore, and be converted, that your sins may be blotted out" (Acts 3:19). You must see the awfulness of sin and then repent of it.

3. *CONFESS:* "If we confess our sins, he is faithful and just to forgive us our sins, and to cleanse us from all unrighteousness" (1 John 1:9). "With the mouth confession is made unto salvation" (Romans 10:10). Confess not to men but to God.

4. *FORSAKE:* "Let the wicked forsake his way, and the unrighteous man his thoughts: and let him return unto the Lord . . . for he will abundantly pardon" (Isaiah 55:7). Sorrow for sin is not

enough in itself. We must want to be done with it once and for all.

5. *BELIEVE:* "For God so loved the world, that he gave his only begotten Son, that whosoever believeth in him should not perish, but have everlasting life" (John 3:16). "If thou shalt confess with thy mouth the Lord Jesus, and shalt believe in thine heart that God hath raised Him from the dead, thou shalt be saved" (Romans 10:9). Believe in the finished work of Christ on the cross.

6. *RECEIVE:* "He came unto his own, and his own received him not. But as many as received him, to them gave he power to become the sons of God, even to them that believe on his name" (John 1:11, 12). Christ must be received personally into the heart by faith, if the experience of the New Birth is to be yours. (FGBMFI)

Faith-Building Messages

by Dave Williams

Cassette Tapes   *$4.00 each**

☐ **S-0504-B**
Side One: *Changing Your God-Given Desires Into Realities!*
Side Two: *The Prevailing Power of Intercessory Prayer*

☐ **H-0505-B**
Side One: *20 Reasons Why Some Are Not Healed*
Side Two: *18 Methods of God's Healing Power*

☐ **G-0518-B**
Side One: *Knowing the Voice of Jesus*
Side Two: *Power of the Imagination*

☐ **G-0601-B**
Side One: *How to Get All Your Needs Met*
Side Two: *Success or Failure — It's Your Choice!*

☐ **K-0010-A**
Side One: *Developing A High Purpose in Life*
Side Two: *3 Keys to Real Achievement*

☐ K-0007-A
Side One: *Developing A Victory Consciousness*
Side Two: *God's Plan for Success That Never Fails*

☐ S-0427-B
Side One: *10 Principles for Successful Church Growth Part 1*
Side Two: *10 Principles for Successful Church Growth Part 2*

☐ P-1230-A
Side One: *Jesus' Life of Prayer*
Side Two: *Reality of the New Creation*

☐ G-0001-A
Side One: *Understanding the Will of God*
Side Two: *Developing the Attitude of Christ*

☐ M-0002-A
Side One: *7 Keys to Finding the Right Mate Part 1*
Side Two: *7 Keys to Finding the Right Mate Part 2*

☐ M-0003-A
Side One: *7 Keys to Finding the Right Mate Part 3*
Side Two: *7 Keys to Finding the Right Mate Part 4*

For tapes, tracts, correspondence courses, books, or special meetings, please write:

Good Ground Evangelical Association
P.O. Box 17115
Lansing, Michigan 48901

*Prices subject to change

ORDER FORM

NAME _____

ADDRESS _____

CITY _____

STATE _____ ZIP _____

QUANTITY	ORDER NO.	TITLE	PRICE	AMOUNT
			TOTAL ENCLOSED	

Please include full amount with each order.

☐ Please send me a free tape listing.
☐ Send order FIRST CLASS. Enclosed is an extra
$2.00.